THE FITZWILLIAM VIRGINAL BOOK

EDITED FROM THE ORIGINAL MANUSCRIPT
WITH AN INTRODUCTION AND NOTES
BY

J. A. FULLER MAITLAND
AND
W. BARCLAY SQUIRE

Revised Dover Edition
Corrected, Edited and with a Preface by

BLANCHE WINOGRON

In Two Volumes
VOLUME I

DOVER PUBLICATIONS, INC.
NEW YORK

Published in Canada by General Publishing Company, Ltd., 30 Lesmill Road, Don Mills, Toronto, Ontario.
Published in the United Kingdom by Constable and Company, Ltd.

The Revised Dover Edition, first published in 1979–80, is an unabridged republication of the work originally published in 1899 by Breitkopf & Härtel that incorporates numerous corrections by Blanche Winogron.
Miss Winogron has written a Preface especially for the Dover Edition in which she comments on the corrections.

International Standard Book Number: 0-486-21068-5
Library of Congress Catalog Card Number: 63-19495

Manufactured in the United States of America
Dover Publications, Inc
180 Varick Street
New York, N.Y. 10014

To

Her Most Gracious Majesty

QUEEN VICTORIA,

EMPRESS OF INDIA,

these volumes

with Her Majesty's permission

are respectfully dedicated

by

Her devoted servants

THE EDITORS.

94
14
15
16
17
Doctor Bull
52
Fantasia

PREFACE TO THE REVISED DOVER EDITION

It is almost eighty years since the distinguished music critic of the London Times, John Alexander Fuller Maitland, and his brother-in-law William Barclay Squire, critic, editor and music librarian of the British Museum, published their impressive transcription of *The Fitzwilliam Virginal Book*. They carried off their difficult task with an astonishing degree of skill and accuracy—a truly monumental accomplishment for the time. Interest in the great *corpus* of English Renaissance music was just beginning; the science of musicology was in its infancy. Impetus for the project may have come from the pioneering activities of Arnold Dolmetsch, a gifted and dynamic Swiss musician, craftsman and indefatigable researcher in early music, newly established in England, whose followers among distinguished musicians, writers and artists included Fuller Maitland. The latter had evidently become an enthusiastic supporter, and a convert to the harpsichord (even to performing in occasional concerts), perhaps inspired by his first acquaintance with the great body of virginal music in the Fitzwilliam Museum uncovered in the process of preparing that institution's music catalog, completed in 1887.

With the tremendous upsurge in the performance of Renaissance and Baroque music in the past forty years, and the serious study of early instruments and their literatures, *The Fitzwilliam Virginal Book* has become recognized as the treasure house of a most sophisticated keyboard music. Highly developed and idiomatic in style, the book is now generally acknowledged to be the foundation for all keyboard music which followed it in the next two centuries. This remarkable collection also serves as an important historical document reflecting the musical life of the time; from this source a large part of English music in many of its facets and forms (including that of the theater) from the 1560s to 1620 could be reconstructed.

Although the Maitland–Squire text has long been accepted as a faithful translation into modern notation (two reprints of the original edition have appeared in the last twenty or more years), a growing number of active performers and scholars have felt that the correction of obvious errors, oversights and misprints (perhaps due to insufficient proofreading) would make it ever more useful. Such lapses were, of course, inevitable considering the enormity and complexity of the publication. However, it was only after a thoroughgoing critical reexamination of the entire collection was undertaken by the present Editor, with a copy of the original manuscript and a pair of virginals at hand, that the full extent and nature of these corrections was realized. There were not only innumerable "lapses," but a considerable number of misreadings and misinterpretations of the manuscript previously unsuspected. Nevertheless a completely new publication was not warranted; needed revision could be successfully accomplished by incorporating the corrections into the existing volumes without altering the basic text, editorial policy or printing style, an operation fortunately made possible by the economical procedures of modern photolithography.

Corrections and changes in this revised edition stem from errors which fall into three categories: those originating with the scribe, those of the printer, and editorial errors in transcription. In the first category we find (a) placement of notes on wrong lines or spaces (a mistake easily made on a six-line staff); wrong placement or omission of clefs and clef changes, or places where these were written so small as to be missed even by the magnifying glass, causing several passages to be transcribed a third too high, too low or in the wrong range (see for example, Volume I, page 66, line 5, measure 2; page 190, line 4, measure 3; Volume II, page 244, line 3, measure 2); (b) many rhythmic and chromatic ambiguities caused by crowding within the measure; omission of dots, stems, tails; uncompleted melodic lines (Volume II, page 39, line 3, measure 1); some illegibility due to age or smudging; and the very nature of the notation itself (see the Introduction, Volume I, pages XI and XII). Printer's errors include occasional omission of, or wrongly placed, modern clefs, fingering, accidentals, stemming, beaming, dots, rests, a few ornaments, some poor alignments, uncompleted melodic lines (sometimes even within a *cantus*—Volume I, page 181, line 3, measure 1).

In a number of cases of editorial misreadings or misinterpretations of notes, rhythms in the manuscript demanded major reconstruction (one or two measures in each instance). The more important of these are: Volume I—page 4, line 5, measure 2; page 20, line 2, measure 4; page 130, line 5, measure 3; page 142, line 2, measure 3; page 171, line 5, measures 2, 3; Volume II—page 23, line 5, measure 1; page 93, line 5, measure 2, line 6, measure 1; page 99, line 3, measure 3; page 265, line 2, measure 1; page 340, line 5, measure 4, line 6, measure 1.

In addition to restoring the many omitted notes (chord

tones, melodic lines), chords, accidentals, rests, and the supplying of editorial brackets and correcting of a few misplaced fingerings, the present Editor has also righted a number of musical decisions (some of them untenable in the light of present-day knowledge) and has clarified occasional confusion among rests, inkblots and *directs*. Indications for triplets and sextolets have been reduced to a minimum for ease of reading, their slurs removed, except when necessary for clarity. Numerals indicating voice entrances in several of the five *Ut, re, mi* pieces have been reduced in size for the sake of consistency and to avoid mistaking them for fingering or numbering of strains. All editorial additions and corrections, except for restoration of what was originally in the manuscript, are bracketed or have footnotes. To preserve the modality of the time, some editorial accidentals have been eliminated and others suggested in parentheses.

Unnecessary footnotes have been emended. In a few places, due to *lacunae* or illegibility of the manuscript, the missing material has been supplied by collation with other manuscripts and is so indicated in footnotes. All fingering is original, a fact only hinted at in the Introduction.

As for the manuscript's elaborate double bars, the original editors recognized their probable decorative function (see the Introduction, Volume I, pages XVI and XVII), but unfortunately decided to include them as repeat signs. They are obviously redundant in the strain and variation form (also traditional in the solo lute and consort music of the time), and have been eliminated throughout except in the short bipartite dances and character pieces without variation, where repeats seem to be called for. In the latter cases, the player may improvise his own simple embellishments. Due to the problem of limited space, first and second endings may not always make mathematical sense when an upbeat is involved; but the player can easily make the necessary adjustment. Final *breve* chords have been retained, since they are more often than not a part of the structural rhythmic pulse.

With reference to the Tregian family connection elaborated on in the Introduction (see pp. VI–IX), the Editor would like to call attention to the most recent findings as published in *Music and Letters:* Cole, Elizabeth, "In Search of Francis Tregian" *(Music and Letters,* XXXIII, 1952, p. 28); Schofield, B. and Dart, T., "Tregian's Anthology" *(Music and Letters,* XXXII, 1951, pp. 205–16).

The critical note to page 373 in Volume I, page XXVI, referring to the *Toccata* of Giovanni Picchi, "This absurd piece of music, by an Italian composer otherwise unknown . . ." should be amended. Picchi (fl. early 17th century) is known to have been organist at the Chiesa Della Casa Grande in Venice. The *Toccata* which represents him in this collection, although not one of his great pieces, is obviously modeled after those of Girolamo Frescobaldi (1583–1643) with whom he probably studied. Picchi's very fine set of twelve dances for keyboard, the *Intavolatura d'Arpicordo* (Venice, 1620), includes a *Pass'e mezzo Antico* and its *Saltarello,* a *Polachca,* two Hungarian dances and a German *Todesca.* He also wrote vocal music, both sacred and secular, and three *Sonatas* for violins and wind instruments.

BLANCHE WINOGRON

January, 1979

INTRODUCTION.

I. HISTORY AND BIBLIOGRAPHY.

The collection of Virginal Music, now printed for the first time, is preserved in the Fitzwilliam Museum, Cambridge, where it has long been erroneously known as "Queen Elizabeth's Virginal Book". It is contained in a small folio volume, consisting of 220 leaves of paper, 209 of which are filled with music, written on six-line staves ruled by hand. The volume measures 33⁹/₁₀ centimetres by 22, and the binding (a fine specimen of English 17th century workmanship) is of crimson morocco, enriched with gold tooling, the sides being sprinkled with fleur-de-lis. The water-mark on the paper is a crozier-case, probably indicating that it came from a manufactory at Basel, the arms of which town bear a similar device. The MS. has in places been cut by the binder, but the style of the work shows that the binding dates from about the same period as the handwriting. Nothing is known of the history of the volume before the early part of the 18th century, when Ward (*Lives of the Gresham Professors*, 1740) printed a list of the compositions by Dr. John Bull contained in it. At this date the book belonged to Dr. Pepusch, from whom Ward derived his information, describing it as a "a large *folio* neatly written, bound in red Turkey leather and guilt." In 1762, at the sale of Pepusch's collection, it was bought for ten guineas by Robert Bremner, from whom it passed to Lord Fitzwilliam, in whose possession it was in 1783. The volume is mentioned in Sir John Hawkins's History of Music (1776) where, for the first time, the statement appears that it belonged originally to Queen Elizabeth. Hawkins is also responsible for the story (repeated by Burney) of Pepusch's wife, Margherita de l'Epine, having attempted to play the music it contained, but, although an excellent performer, never being able to master the first piece, Bull's variations on "Walsingham". Burney (*Hist. of Mus. III, 14*) adds the account from Sir James Melvil's "Memoirs" of Queen Elizabeth's performance upon the virginals, with the remark that "if Her Majesty was ever able to execute any of the pieces that are preserved in a MS. which goes under the name of *Queen Elizabeth's Virginal Book*, she must have been a very great player, as some of the pieces are so difficult that it would be hardly possible to find a master in Europe who would undertake to play one of them at the end of a month's practice." Bur-

EINLEITUNG.

Deutsche Übersetzung von *John Bernhoff.*

I. ENTSTEHUNGSGESCHICHTE DER SAMMLUNG UND QUELLENANGABE.

Die Sammlung der jetzt zum erstenmal im Druck erscheinenden Kompositionen für das *Virginal* liegt im Fitzwilliam-Museum zu Cambridge (England) aufbewahrt, wo dieselbe lange fälschlicherweise als das »Queen Elizabeth's Virginal Book« bekannt war. Sie ist in einem kleinen aus 220 Papierblättern bestehenden Folio-Band enthalten, von welchen 209 mit Kompositionen angefüllt sind. Diese Kompositionen sind auf einem mit freier Hand gezogenen, sechsreihigen Notensystem geschrieben. Das Buch ist 33⁹/₁₀ cm lang und 22 cm breit. Der Einband (ein Prachtexemplar englischer Buchbinderkunst des 17. Jahrhunderts) ist aus carmoisinrotem Marokkoleder, mit Goldabdrücken, gefertigt; die Decken sind mit fleur-de-lis reich verziert. Das Wasserzeichen des Papiers stellt ein Bischofsstabfutteral dar, woraus man wohl schliessen darf, dass es aus einer Baseler Fabrik stammt, da das Stadtwappen von Basel ein ähnliches Sinnbild aufweist. Das Manuskript ist stellenweise vom Buchbinder beschnitten worden, jedoch verrät der Charakter der Arbeit, dass Einband und Handschrift ungefähr derselben Zeit entstammen. Erst gegen Anfang des 18. Jahrhunderts wurde die Vorgeschichte des Bandes bekannt, als Ward (in seinem Werke: »*Lives of the Gresham Professors*«, 1740) ein Verzeichnis der darin enthaltenen Kompositionen von Dr. John Bull zum Abdruck brachte. Damals gehörte das Buch Dr. Pepusch, von dem Ward seine Kenntnisse über das Werk schöpfte, indem er es als: »ein Gross-**folio**-Band, schön geschrieben, in rot Saffian gebunden und vergoldet«, beschreibt. Im Jahre 1762 wurde es in der Auktion der Pepuschsammlung von Robert Bremner für zehn guineas*) käuflich erworben; von diesem ging das Werk auf Lord Fitzwilliam über, in dessen Besitz es sich im Jahre 1783 befand. Das Buch wird in Sir John Hawkins »*History of Music*« (1776) erwähnt, wo zum erstenmal ausgesagt wird, dass es ursprünglich der Königin Elisabeth angehört habe. Hawkins ist auch verantwortlich für die Geschichte (welche Burney wiederholt), dass die Frau von Pepusch, Margherita de l'Epine, versucht habe, die darin enthaltenen Kompositionen zu spielen; dass sie indessen nicht im stande war, das erste Stück, Bull's Variationen über »Walsingham«, zu bewältigen, obgleich sie eine vorzügliche Spielerin war. In

*) Circa 210 Mark.

ney's remarks have been repeated by several writers, amongst others by Steevens, in his notes to Shakespeare's "Winter's Tale" (1803), but until the appearance of Mr. Chappell's "Ballad Literature and Popular Music of the Olden Time" (1859) no further attention seems to have been paid to the history of the manuscript, although Warren inserted an inaccurate list of its contents in the notes to the life of William Byrd in his edition of Boyce's "Cathedral Music" (1849). Mr. Chappell surmised that the collection might have been made for or by an English resident in the Netherlands and that Dr. Pepusch obtained it in that country. This conjecture he founded upon the fact that the only name which occurs in an abbreviated form throughout the book is that of Tregian, and that a sonnet signed "Fr. Tregian" is prefixed to Richard Verstegan's "Restitution of Decayed Intelligence", which was published at Antwerp in 1605. The name occurs as follows: on p. 111 (vol. i. p. 226) is a composition by William Byrd headed "Treg. Ground", on p. 152 (vol. i. p. 321) is a Pavan by Peter Phillips, dated 1593 and entitled "Pavana Dolorosa. Treg." on p. 171 (vol. i. p. 367) the initials "Ph. Tr." head a Pavan of Byrd's; on p. 297 (vol. ii. p. 237) the initials "F. Tr." are written against a Jig by Byrd; and on p. 315 (vol. ii. p. 278) "Mrs. Katherin Tregian's Pavan" is written in the margin of a "Pavana Chromatica" by William Tisdall. Mention may also be made of the fact that the syllable "Fre." (a not impossible abbreviation of "F. Tregian") occurs as the name of the composer of "Heaven and Earth" p. 196 (vol i. p. 415), and that on p. 278 (see note to vol. ii. p. 190) is the marginal note "300 to S. T. by Tom", — a possible reminder to the writer that "Tom" was to take "300" to S. Tregian, who may have been the Sybil Tregian mentioned in a letter from Benjamin Tichborne to Lord Keeper Pickering preserved at the Record Office. (*Calendar of State Papers, Dom. Ser. Elizabeth. CCXLVIII, no. 118*, quoted by Morris, "*Troubles of our Catholic Forefathers*", *Second Series, p. 143*). These few clues certainly seem to point to some connection of the volume with the Tregians*) who were a rich and powerful Catholic

*) The following are the authorities from which the account of the Tregian family has been derived: Oliver: "Catholic Religion in Cornwall" 1857, p. 203); Polwhele's "History of Cornwall" (1866), IV. 88—90, V. 156; Catholic Miscellany for June, 1823; Morris, "Troubles of our Catholic Forefathers" (1872—1877), First Series; Knox, "Records of the English Catholics" (1878—1882) I., II.; Gilbert, "Historical Survey of Cornwall" (1817) II., 281; "The Oeconomy of the Fleete" edited for the Camden Society (1879) by Jessopp, p. 140; "A Briefe Note concerning the Proceeding and Course held against Francis Tregian" (British Museum, Add. Ms. 21, 203); Murray's Guide to Portugal (1887), p. 21: Calendars of State Papers, Dom. Series, James I., 1619, Add. Vol. 41, no. 116 and 1620 no. 116; Historical MSS. Commission, House of Lords, Sup. Cal. Report IV. (1874) p. 120; ditto. Marquis of Salisbury's papers, Report VI. Appendix (1877) p. 272a, Report VII. (1879) p. 185b.

seinem Werke: »*History of Music*« (Vol. III. p. 14) berichtet Burney aus Sir James Melvils »*Memoirs*« über Königin Elisabeths Leistungen auf dem Virginal, und bemerkt: »Wenn Ihre Majestät jemals im stande war, irgendwelche der Stücke, die in einem Manuskript, das unter dem Titel: ‚Queen Elizabeth's Virginal-Book' bekannt ist, zu spielen, so muss sie eine grossartige Spielerin gewesen sein, da einzelne der Stücke so schwer sind, dass man in ganz Europa kaum einen Meister finden würde, der es übernähme, auch nur eines davon zu spielen, und übte er einen Monat daran«. Burneys Worte sind von mehreren Schriftstellern wiederholt worden, unter anderen von Stevens in seinen Erläuterungen zu Shakespeares »Winter-Märchen« (1803); aber bis Mr. Chappells »*Ballad Literature and Popular Music of the Olden Time*« (1859) herauskam, scheint der Entstehungsgeschichte des Manuskripts keine weitere Aufmerksamkeit gewidmet worden zu sein, trotzdem Warren seiner Ausgabe von Boyce's »*Cathedral Music*« 1849, unter Bemerkungen zu dem Leben von William Byrd ein (zwar) ungenaues Verzeichnis seines Inhalts beifügte. Mr. Chappell vermutete, dass die Sammlung möglicherweise für einen, oder von einem in den Niederlanden wohnenden Engländer gemacht worden wäre, und dass Dr. Pepusch dort in den Besitz des Werks gelangt sei. Die Vermutung beruht auf der Thatsache, dass »Tregian« der einzige im ganzen Buche, in abgekürzter Form vorkommende Name, und dass ein Sonett, unterschrieben »Fr. Tregian« dem in Antwerpen 1605 veröffentlichten Werke des Richard Verstegan, betitelt: »*Restitution of Decayed Intelligence*« vorangesetzt ist. Der Name kommt in folgenden Formen und Abkürzungen vor: auf S. 111 (Band 1. S. 226) steht eine Komposition von William Byrd, überschrieben: »Treg. Ground«; auf S.152 (Band 1. S. 321) eine Pavane von Peter Philips mit der Jahreszahl 1593 versehen und betitelt: Pavana Dolorosa Treg.«; auf S. 171 (Band 1. S. 367) stehen die Anfangsbuchstaben »Ph. Tr.« über einer Pavane von Byrd; auf S. 297 (Band 2. S. 237) stehen die Anfangsbuchstaben »F. Tr.« bei einer Gigue von Byrd, und auf S. 315 (Band 2. S. 278) steht: »Mrs. Katherin Tregian's Pavan« am Rande einer »Pavana Chromatica« von William Tisdall geschrieben. Es ist hierbei noch zu erwähnen, dass die Silbe »Fre.« (möglicherweise eine Abkürzung von F. Tregian) als Name des Komponisten von »Heaven and Earth« auf S. 196 (Band 1. S. 415) vorkommt, und dass auf S. 278 (siehe Anmerkung zu Band 2. S. 190) die Randglosse »300 to S. T. by Tom« *) steht. Sollte dieses etwa den Verfasser daran erinnern, dass Thomas »300« zu S. Tregian hintragen sollte, vielleicht zu Sybil Tregian, welche in einem Briefe von Benjamin Tichborne an Lord Keeper Pickering erwähnt wird; dieses Schriftstück befindet sich im Record Office zu London. (*Calendar of State Papers, Dom. Ser. Elizabeth. CCXLVIII. No. 118*, angeführt von Morris, »*Troubles of our Catholic Forefathers*« Second Series, p. 134). Diese wenigen Anhaltspunkte scheinen auf eine Beziehung des Buches zu den Tregians zu deuten,**)

*) "300 an S. T. von Thomas".

**) Quellen, denen der Bericht über die Tregian Familie entnommen sind: Oliver: "Catholic Religion in Cornwall" 1857, p. 203); Polwhele's "History of Cornwall" (1866), IV. 88—90, V. 156; Catholic Miscellany for June, 1823; Morris, "Troubles of our Catholic Forefathers" (1872—1877), First Series; Knox, "Records of the English Catholics (1878—1882) I., II.; Gilbert, Historical Survey of Cornwall" (1817) II., 281; "The Oeconomy of the Fleete" edited for the Camden Society (1879) by Jessopp, p, 140; "A Briefe Note concerning the Proceeding and Course held against Francis Tregian" (British Museum, Add. Ms. 21, 203); Murray's Guide to Portugal (1887), p. 21: Calendars of State Papers, Dom. Series, James I., 1619, Add. vol. 41, no. 116 and 1620, no. 116; Historical MSS. Commission, House of Lords, Sup. Cal. Report IV. (1874) p. 120; ditto. Marquis of Salisbury's papers, Report VI. appendix (1877) p. 272a, Report VII. (1879) p. 185b.

family, and whose seat was at Golden or Volveden, in the parish of Probus, near Trewithen, where the remains of their house still exist.

Towards the close of the 16th. century the head of the family was named Francis Tregian; he was the son of Thomas Tregian and Catherine, daughter of Sir John Arundell of Lanherne, and his wife was Mary, daughter of Charles, Lord Stourton. In the year 1577 the members of the Tregian family seem to have become suspected, probably as much on account of their wealth as of their religion, and (according to one account) a conspiracy was planned for their ruin. On June 8 the house at Golden was searched and a young priest of Douay, Cuthbert Mayne, who acted as steward to Francis Tregian, was arrested and imprisoned, together with several of the household servants. At the following assizes, Mayne was convicted of high treason and on Nov. 29 of the same year he was executed with hideous barbarity at Launceston. Mayne was the first priest to suffer under the long persecution which the English Catholics endured during the reigns of Elizabeth and James I., and his name was included in the list of martyrs beatified by Leo XIII. in 1886. Tregian himself, who had been bound over to appear at the assizes, was committed a close prisoner to the Marshalsea, where he remained for ten months. He was then suddenly arraigned before the King's Bench and sent into Cornwall to be tried. For some time the jury would deliver no verdict, but after having been repeatedly threatened by the judges, a conviction was obtained, and Tregian was sentenced to suffer the penalty of *praemunire* and perpetual banishment. On hearing his sentence he exclaimed: "Pereant bona, quae si non periissent, fortassis dominum suum perdidissent!" Immediately judgement was given, he was laden with irons and thrown into the common county-gaol; his goods were seized, his wife and children were expelled from their home and his mother was deprived of her jointure. After being moved from prison to prison and suffering indignities without number, Tregian was finally confined in the Fleet, where his wife joined him. He remained in prison for twenty-four years, during which time he suffered much from illness, occupying himself by writing poetry. In 1601 he petitioned from the Fleet that for his health and upon good security being given he might "have the benefit of the open air about London (not exceeding five miles circuit), yielding his body every night to the Fleet", and also for leave on certain conditions to visit Buxton or Bath, having of late been "grievously punished with Sciatica". His petition seems to have been granted, for on 25 July 1602, he wrote from Chelsea to Sir Robert Cecil to the effect that the day on which, through the Queen's clemency, he came from the Fleet to Chelsea, he was "enriched with a litter of greyhound whelps"; a brace of which he designed for Cecil, they being now just a year old. In 1606 he left England and went to Madrid, visiting (July 1606) Douay on his way. In Spain he was kindly received by Philip III., who granted him a pension. He retired to Lisbon, where he died Sept. 25, 1608, aged 60. He was buried under the left pulpit in the church of St. Roque, where a long inscription to his memory is still to be seen. At Lisbon he soon came to be regarded as a saint; his body was said to have been found uncorrupted twenty years after his

welche eine begüterte, einflussreiche, katholische Familie waren und ihren Wohnsitz in Golden oder Volveden, Bezirk Probus bei Trewithen hatten, wo die Ruinen ihres Hauses noch zu sehen sind.

Das Haupt der Familie gegen Ende des 16. Jahrhunderts hiess Francis Tregian, Sohn von Thomas und Catherine Tregian, letztere die Tochter von Sir John Arundell of Lanherne. Die Gattin des Francis war Mary, Tochter von Charles, Lord Stourton. Im Jahre 1577 scheinen die Mitglieder der Tregian-Familie wohl ihres Reichtums so sehr wie ihrer Religion wegen verdächtigt worden zu sein, und, nach einem Bericht, wurde eine Verschwörung geplant, sie zu vernichten. Am 8. Juni liess man das Haus zu Golden durchsuchen, einen jungen Priester aus Douay, Cuthbert Mayne, der die Stelle eines Haushofmeisters bei Francis Tregian vertrat, mit mehreren der Bedienten verhaften und in's Gefängnis werfen. Beim nächsten Assisengericht erklärte man Mayne des Hochverrats schuldig, und er wurde am 29. November desselben Jahres zu Launceston auf die brutalste Weise hingerichtet. Mayne war der erste Priester, der während der langen Verfolgung, welche die englischen Katholiken unter der Regierung Elisabeths und Jakobs I. erduldeten, den Tod erlitt. Sein Name wurde in die Liste der von Leo XIII. im Jahre 1886 heilig gesprochenen Märtyrer eingetragen. Tregian, welcher sich hatte verpflichten müssen, selbst beim Assisengericht zu erscheinen, wurde als streng bewachter Gefangener ins Marshalsea-Gefängnis zu London geschickt, wo er zehn Monate blieb. Dann stellte man ihn plötzlich vor das King's Bench-Gericht, von wo er nach Cornwall kam, um dort verhört zu werden. Eine zeitlang weigerten sich die Geschworenen, ein Urteil zu fällen; nachdem aber die Richter ihnen wiederholt gedroht hatten, wurde Tregian schuldig gesprochen. Man erklärte ihn seiner Güter verlustig, und verurteilte ihn zu lebenslänglicher Verbannung. Als er sein Urteil vernahm, rief er aus: »Pereant bona, quae si non periissent, fortassis dominum suum perdidissent!« Sowie der Richterspruch gefallen war, wurde er in Eisenfesseln geschlagen und in das gemeine Provinzialgefängnis geworfen. Man konfiszierte seine Güter; sein Weib, seine Kinder wurden aus ihrem Heim vertrieben und seine Mutter ward ihres Wittums beraubt. Aus einem Gefängnis in das andere geworfen, und nachdem er eine Erniedrigung nach der anderen erduldet hatte, kam Tregian als Gefangener in das Fleet-Gefängnis zu London, wohin ihm seine Frau folgte. Vierundzwanzig Jahre brachte er so im Gefängnis zu, während welcher Zeit er viel mit Krankheit zu kämpfen hatte, und sich mit poetischen Arbeiten beschäftigte. Im Jahre 1601 reichte er eine Bittschrift ein, in welcher er bat, dass man ihm gestatte, seine angegriffene Gesundheit in der Umgebung Londons (nicht über fünf englische Meilen im Umkreise) wiederherzustellen, wogegen er sich verpflichte, sich jede Nacht im Gefängnisse zu stellen; ferner unter gewissen Bedingungen, den Badeort Buxton oder Bath zu besuchen, da er in letzter Zeit an schwerer Ischias zu leiden gehabt hätte. Man scheint ihm die Bitte gewährt zu haben, denn am 25. Juli 1602 schrieb er von Chelsea aus an Sir Robert Cecil, dass er, an dem Tage, an welchem durch die Güte der Königin er vom Fleet-Gefängnis nach Chelsea gekommen war, durch einen Wurf junger Windspiele bereichert worden sei. Von diesen, da sie jetzt gerade ein Jahr alt wären, bestimmte er ein Paar für Cecil. Im Jahre 1606 verliess er England und ging nach Madrid, indem er (im

death, and it was alleged that miracles had been worked at his grave. Francis Tregian had no fewer than eighteen children, eleven of whom were born while he was in prison. The eldest son, who bore his father's name of Francis, was educated first at Eu and entered the college of Douay 29 Sept. 1586. On the occasion of a visit of the Bishop of Piacenza (14 Aug. 1591) he was chosen to deliver a Latin address of welcome. He left Douay on 11 July, 1592 and was afterwards for two years chamberlain to Cardinal Allen, upon whose death in 1594 he delivered a funeral oration in the church of the English College at Rome. This was the probably the "Planctus de Morte Cardinalis Alani" which, according to some accounts, was written by Charles Tregian, another son of the elder Francis Tregian. In a list of the Cardinal's household, drawn up after his death and now preserved in the archives of Simancas, Francis Tregian the younger is described as "molto nobile, di 20 anni, secolare, di ingenio felicissimo, dotto in filosofia, in musica, et nella lingua latina". In a draft petition of the year 1614, preserved in the House of Lords, it is stated that he had borne arms against the friends of Queen Elizabeth, but eventually he returned to England, where he bought back some of his father's lands. The details of the transaction are somewhat obscure, but it seems to have led to his being convicted in 1608—9 of recusancy, and to his imprisonment in the Fleet, where he remained until his death, about 1619. From a statement drawn up by the Warden of the Fleet prison (apparently about 1622), it seems that at his death he owed over £200 for meat, drink and lodging, though in his rooms there were many hundreds of books, the ownership of which formed a matter of dispute between his sisters and the Warden. It may be conjectured with much plausibility that the present collection of music was written by the younger Tregian to wile away his time in prison. The latest dated composition it contains is the "*Ut, re, mi, fa, sol, la*" by the Amsterdam organist Sweelinck, which bears the date 1612, while the series of dated pieces by Peter Philips, who was an English Catholic ecclesiastic settled in the Netherlands, the note to Byrd's Pavan, before referred to, and the heading of Bull's Jig*), all point to the conclusion that the collection was formed by someone who was intimate with the Catholic refugees of the period. In this respect the evidence of Philips's pieces is especially important, as MSS. by him are hardly ever found in contemporary collections formed in England. The handwriting also bears out the theory that the MS. was written in the manner suggested; though obviously proceeding throughout from the same hand, the characters gradually become larger as the work goes on. In the absence of any undoubted specimen of the younger Tregian's writing, the point must remain for the present unsettled. Search has been made in the records of the diocese of Westminster, the English Colleges at Douay and Rome, the Vatican and other libraries, but no trace of Tregian's writing has yet been discovered. In the accounts of the collection which have appeared in Grove's Dictionary of Music and Musicians, III. 305—310) and the Catalogue of the Music in the Fitzwilliam Museum (1893, pp. 104—119) in which the attempt

*) Bull fled to the Netherlands in 1613.

Juli 1606) Douay auf dem Wege dahin berührte. In Spanien wurde er von Philipp III. freundlich aufgenommen, und wurde ihm von diesem König eine Pension gewährt. Er zog sich nach Lissabon zurück, wo er am 25. September 1608, im Alter von 60 Jahren starb. Man setzte seine Leiche unter der linken Kanzel in der Kirche zu St. Roque bei, wo noch heute eine lange, seinem Andenken gewidmete Inschrift sich befindet. In Lissabon wurde er bald als Heiliger verehrt; die Leiche soll zwanzig Jahre nach seinem Tode noch unversehrt geblieben, und an seinem Grabe sollen Wunder gewirkt worden sein. Francis Tregian hatte nicht weniger als achtzehn Kinder, von denen elf während seines Aufenthaltes im Gefängnis geboren wurden. Der älteste nach dem Vater benannte Sohn, Francis, erhielt seine erste Erziehung zu Eu, und trat am 29. September 1586 in das Kollegium zu Douay ein. Gelegentlich eines Besuchs des Bischofs von Piacenza (14. August 1591) wurde er dazu auserlesen, eine lateinische Begrüssungsrede zu halten. Am 11. Juli 1592 verliess er Douay, und war später zwei Jahre lang Kämmerling des Kardinals Allen, bei dessen Tode er eine Leichenrede in der Kirche des »English College« zu Rom hielt. Dies war wahrscheinlich der »*Planctus de Morte Cardinalis Alani*«, welcher nach den Aussagen einiger von Charles Tregian, einem anderen Sohne von Francis Tregian (Vater) geschrieben sein soll. In einem Verzeichnis des Haushalts des Kardinals, welches nach seinem Tode abgefasst wurde, und jetzt in den Archiven von Simancas aufbewahrt ist, wird Francis Tregian der Jüngere folgendermassen beschrieben: »molto nobile, di 20 anni, secolare, di ingenio felicissimo, dotto in filosofia, in musica et nella lingua latina«. In dem Entwurf einer Bittschrift aus dem Jahre 1614, jetzt im House of Lords aufbewahrt, steht, dass er Waffen gegen die Freunde der Königin Elisabeth geführt habe; aber schliesslich nach England zurückgekehrt sei, wo er einen Teil der Ländereien seines Vaters zurückgekauft habe. Die Einzelheiten der Verhandlung sind etwas in Dunkel gehüllt; jedoch scheint die Sache dahin geführt zu haben, dass er zwischen den Jahren 1608 bis 1609, der Abtrünnigkeit überführt, als Gefangener dem Fleet-Gefängnis übergeben wurde, wo er bis zu seinem ca. im Jahre 1619 erfolgten Tode blieb. Nach einem von dem Gefängniswärter ca. 1622 abgefassten Bericht scheint er bei seinem Tode über £ 200 für Fleisch, Getränke und Wohnung schuldig gewesen zu sein, obgleich sich in seinen Zimmern viele Hunderte von Büchern befanden, deren Eigentumsrecht von seinen Schwestern und dem Wärter bestritten wurde. Man kann mit grosser Wahrscheinlichkeit annehmen, dass die heutige Musiksammlung von dem jüngeren Tregian geschrieben wurde, der sich damit die Zeit im Gefängnis zu vertreiben suchte. Die darin zuletzt datierte Komposition ist die »*Ut, re, mi, fa, sol, la*« von dem Amsterdamer Organisten Sweelinck. Sie trägt die Jahreszahl 1612, während die Serie der mit Jahreszahl versehenen Stücke von Peter Philips, einem in den Niederlanden angesiedelten englischen katholischen Geistlichen, zu dem Schlusse nötigt, dass die Sammlung von jemandem, der mit den damaligen katholischen Flüchtlingen auf intimem Fusse stand, angelegt wurde. Zu gleichem Schlusse zwingen die Anmerkung zu Byrd's Pavane, auf die wir vorhin Bezug nahmen, und die Überschrift zu Bull's Gigue.*) In dieser Beziehung liefern die Philip-

*) Bull ist i. J. 1613 nach den Niederlanden geflüchtet.

was first made to develop Mr. Chappell's suggestion that the MS. was connected the Tregian family, it was stated that there was an insuperable difficulty to the younger Francis Tregian's claim to have been the transcriber, owing to the existence of evidence that much of the volume at least must have been written after the date of his death. No. CXXXVIII of the collection (vol. ii. p. 128) is a short composition by Dr. John Bull entitled "D. Bull's Juell", and another copy of it was said to occur at fol. 49b of a manuscript collection of Bull's instrumental music in the British Museum (Add. MSS. 23,623) with the heading "Het Juweel van Doctor Jan Bull, quod fecit anno 1621 : 12 December." The Museum MS. is especially valuable as containing several dated compositions of Bull's, and this evidence seemed conclusive against the theory that the collection could have been written by the younger Tregian during the imprisonment which ended with his death about 1619. The publication of the Virginal Book, however, has enabled a further comparison to be made of its contents with those of the MS. in question, from which it turns out that the composition of 1621 is not the same as the "D. Bull's Juell" here printed, but a totally different setting of the same tune. The Virginal Book version, moreover, occurs, with some additions, at fol. 70b, of the Museum MS. as "Courante Juweel: van Jan Bull, Doct.", but without any date as to when it was composed. This new evidence, therefore, is of importance as removing what seemed the main difficulty to the theory of the origin of the MS. in the Fleet prison.

The history of the Virginal Book from the date at which it must have been written until its appearance in the collection of Dr. Pepusch is absolutely a blank. That it was highly treasured by an early owner is evident from the costly binding in which it was placed. The passage already referred to in the statement of the Warden of the Fleet, proves that Tregian's sisters were anxious to secure his books, and it may well be supposed that it was owing to the value placed upon it by one of them that the volume has been handed down in its present condition. But of the

schen Stücke ein besonders wichtiges Beweismaterial, da MSS. von ihm fast niemals in den in England gemachten zeitgenössischen Sammlungen sich vorfinden. Die Handschrift rechtfertigt die Annahme, dass das MS. in der angedeuteten Weise geschrieben wurde; und obgleich es unstreitig von Anfang bis Ende von derselben Hand herrührt, werden die Schriftzeichen mit dem Fortgang des Werkes immer grösser. Da wir kein Schriftstück besitzen, von welchem es zweifellos feststeht, dass es von der Hand des jüngeren Tregian geschrieben ist, muss dieser Punkt einstweilen unerwiesen bleiben. Man hat in den Archiven der Diöcese von Westminster, in den englischen Kollegien zu Douay und Rom, im Vatikan und in anderen Bibliotheken nachgeforscht; bis jetzt ist nirgends die Spur einer Tregian-Handschrift aufgetaucht. In den Berichten über die Sammlung, welche in Grove's »*Dictionary of Music and Musicians*« (Bd. 3. S. 305 bis 310), und in dem »*Catalogue of the Music in the Fitzwilliam-Museum*« (1893. S. 104—119) erschienen sind, — und wo der Versuch zuerst gemacht wurde, W. Chappells Behauptung, dass das MS. mit der Tregian-Familie in Verbindung stände, weiter zu führen, — stand, dass des jüngeren Tregians Anspruch darauf, der Abschreiber gewesen zu sein, insofern auf eine unüberwindliche Schwierigkeit stosse, als Beweismaterial vorhanden sei, aus welchem hervorgehe, dass wenigstens ein grosser Teil des Bandes erst nach dem Datum seines Todes geschrieben worden sein müsse. Nr. CXXXVIII der Sammlung (Bd. 2. S. 128) ist eine kurze Komposition von Dr. John Bull, betitelt »D. Bull's Juell«, und eine weitere Abschrift derselben sollte auf fol. 49b einer Handschriftensammlung von Bulls Instrumentalmusik im *British Museum* (Add. MS. 23. 623) überschrieben: »Het Juweel van Doctor Jan Bull, quod fecit anno 1621: 12. December«, vorkommen. Das Museum MS. hat dadurch besonderen Wert, dass es mehrere mit Datum versehene Kompositionen von Bull enthält, und dieses Zeugnis schien endgültig gegen die Annahme zu sprechen, dass die Sammlung von dem jüngeren Tregian während der erst mit seinem (ca. 1619 stattgefundenen) Tode endenden Gefangenschaft geschrieben sein konnte. Die Herausgabe des »Virginal Book« hat aber einen Vergleich seines Inhalts mit dem des in Frage stehenden MS. ermöglicht, aus welchem hervorgeht, dass die Komposition von 1621 nicht dieselbe ist, wie die hier abgedruckte D. Bull's Juell, sondern eine ganz andere Bearbeitung derselben Melodie. Die Komposition, wie sie übrigens im »Virginal Book« vorkommt, befindet sich mit einigen Hinzufügungen auf fol. 70b des Museum MS., betitelt: »Courante Juweel: van Jan Bull, Doct.«, jedoch ohne Datum bezüglich der Zeit ihrer Komposition. Dieses neue Zeugnis ist daher insofern von Wichtigkeit, als es das, was scheinbar die Hauptschwierigkeit bot gegen die Annahme, das MS. sei in dem Fleet-Gefängnis entstanden, beseitigt.

Die Geschichte des »Virginal Book«, von der Zeit an, in welcher es geschrieben worden sein muss, bis zu seinem Erscheinen in Dr. Pepusch's Sammlung, ist absolut unbekannt. Der Umstand, dass der frühe Besitzer es so kostbar einbinden liess, zeugt dafür, dass er es hochschätzte. Die Stelle in dem Bericht des Gefängniswärters, auf welche wir uns schon bezogen, beweist, dass es Tregian's Schwestern sehr darum zu thun war, sich seine Bücher zu sichern; und es ist wohl anzunehmen, dass wir es dem Wert, welchen eine von ihnen auf den Band legte, zu verdanken haben, dass uns

subsequent fate of the Tregian family and of the younger Tregian's seventeen brothers and sisters hardly anything is known. One of his sisters, Mary Tregian, married a Thomas Yates of Berkshire, another (whose name is unknown) became the wife of a Francis Plunkett, who in 1655 wrote an account of his father-in-law's life; the husband of a third sister was named Haweis; of the brothers nothing is known, and the family seems to have utterly died out.

A few words remain to be said about the composers who are represented in the collection. For biographical details concerning most of them reference to the Dictionary of National Biography will give all the information at present accessible, but the following additional particulars may not be out of place. Jan Pieterson Sweelinck was the greatest Dutch composer of his time, and particulars of his life will be found in the "Tijdschrift" of the "Vereeniging voor Noord-Nederlands Muziekgeschiedenis", which Society is also now (1899) publishing a complete edition of his works. His connection with the English instrumental composers of his day is a subject of much interest, which has been fully dealt with by his learned biographer and editor, Dr. Max Seiffert. Further details of the life of John Dowland, including the curious story of his early adoption of the Roman Catholic faith, will be found in the "Musical Times" for December 1896 and February 1897. The same article also contains some corrections of the biography of Robert Johnson contained in the "Dictionary of National Biography", in which it is erroneously stated that "Dr. Wilson described him as a musician of Shakespeare's company" and Dr. Rimbault's theory is adopted that he was in 1574 in the service of Sir Thomas Kytson of Hengrave, whereas in reality he was the son of John Johnson, one of Queen Elizabeth's musicians, and in 1576 was apprenticed for seven years to Sir George Carey. Marchant was a musician in the service of Lady Arabella Stuart. William Inglott was born in 1554 and was appointed organist of Hereford in 1597. He left there probably about 1607, for in 1608 he was organist of Norwich, where he remained until his death in 1621. He is buried in the cathedral, where his epitaph states that

> "For Descant most, for Voluntary all
> He past, on Organ, Song and Virginall."

Ferdinando Richardson was the name by which Sir Ferdinando Heyborne was known in the earlier part of his life. He was born about 1558 and studied music under Thomas Tallis, as may be gathered from the Latin verses by him prefixed to the "Sacrae Cantiones" of Byrd and Tallis, published in 1575. Heyborne can never have been more than an amateur musician, for in 1587 he was appointed a groom of the Privy Chamber to Queen Elizabeth, an office he held until 1611, when he retired with a pension of 100 marks. He married (1) Ann, daughter and heiress of Richard Candeler, of London; and (2) Elizabeth, daughter of Francis More, of Sussex. Sir Ferdinando died 4 June, 1618, aged 60, and is buried in the Parish Church of Tottenham, Middlesex, where there is a monument to his memory, bearing his effigy with that of his first wife and her father and mother. (*Calendars of State Papers, Dom. Ser. Elizabeth and James I.*

derselbe in seinem heutigen Zustande erhalten blieb. Von den späteren Schicksalen der Tregian-Familie, und den siebzehn Geschwistern des jüngeren Tregian ist fast nichts bekannt. Eine der Schwestern, Mary Tregian, heiratete einen Thomas Yates aus Berkshire; eine andere (deren Vorname uns unbekannt ist) wurde die Frau eines Francis Plunkett, der im Jahre 1655 das Leben seines Schwiegervaters beschrieb. Der Mann einer dritten Schwester hiess Haweis; von den Brüdern wissen wir nichts; die Familie scheint ausgestorben zu sein.

Einige Worte über die in der Sammlung vertretenen Komponisten dürfen hier wohl angebracht sein. Biographische Abrisse über die meisten von ihnen bietet das »*Dictionary of National Biography*«, d. h. soweit Einzelheiten aus ihrem Leben bis jetzt bekannt sind. Wir fügen folgendes hinzu: Jan Pieterson Sweelinck war der grösste holländische Komponist seiner Zeit, und Näheres über sein Leben befindet sich in der »Tijdschrift« der »Vereeniging voor Noord-Nederlands Muziekgeschiedenis«, welche Gesellschaft jetzt (1899) eine vollständige Auflage seiner Werke herausgiebt. Seine Beziehungen zu den zeitgenössischen englischen Instrumentalkomponisten bietet viel Interessantes, und sein gelehrter Biograph und Herausgeber Dr. Max Seiffert hat diesen Gegenstand völlig erschöpft. Näheres über das Leben John Dowland's und die interessante Geschichte seines frühen Übertritts zum Katholicismus, befindet sich in der »Musical Times«, December 1896 und Februar 1897. Derselbe Artikel verbessert einiges aus der in dem »Dictionary of National Biography« enthaltenen Biographie von Robert Johnson, in welcher irrtümlich steht, dass »Dr. Wilson ihn als einen Musiker aus Shakespeare's Gesellschaft schildert«, und wo die Aussage von Dr. Rimbault wiederholt wird, dass er im Jahre 1754 im Dienste von Sir Thomas Kytson aus Hengrave gestanden habe. In Wirklichkeit war er der Sohn von John Johnson, einem der Musiker der Königin Elisabeth. Er kam 1576 auf sieben Jahre in die Lehre bei Sir George Carey. Marchant war Musiker im Dienste der Lady Arabella Stuart.

William Inglott wurde 1554 geboren und im Jahre 1597 zum Organisten von Hereford ernannt. Wahrscheinlich ging er circa 1607 von da fort, denn 1608 war er Organist von Norwich, wo er bis zu seinem im Jahre 1621 stattgefundenen Tod blieb. Er ist im Dome begraben, und auf seinem Grabe steht:

> "For Descant most, for Voluntary all
> He past, on Organ, Song and Virginall." *)

Ferdinando Richardson lautet der Name, unter welchem Sir Ferdinando Heyborne als junger Mann bekannt war. Er wurde circa 1558 geboren und studierte Musik unter Thomas Tallis, wie hervorgeht aus den von ihm auf Lateinisch abgefassten Versen, welche den im Jahre 1575 herausgegebenen »*Sacrae Cantiones*« von Byrd und Tallis vorangesetzt sind. Heyborne kann niemals mehr als Dilettant gewesen sein, denn im Jahre 1587 wurde er zum »groom of the Privy Chamber« **) der Königin Elisabeth ernannt, welches Amt er bis zum Jahre 1611 bekleidete, als er sich mit einer Pension von 100 Mark zurückzog. Er heiratete 1) Ann, Tochter und

*) Diese Grabschrift dürfte in die heutige Sprache frei übersetzt wohl so viel heissen wie: Als Improvisator und im Vortrag geschriebener Stücke oder Soli übertraf er alle oder die meisten Zeitgenossen, sowohl in Gesangs- als in Instrumental-Musik.

**) Kammerdiener.

Robinson, History of Tottenham, [1840] II. 42.) Thomas Warrock, or Warwick, was a descendant of an old Cumberland family. He was appointed organist of Hereford 30 Sept. 1586, a post he only retained fcr three years. He married Elizabeth, daughter of John Somerville of Aston Somerville, Gloucester, and by her was the father of Sir Philip Warwick, (b. at Westminster, 24 Dec. 1609). In 1625 he succeded Orlando Gibbons as organist of the Chapel Royal, but in 1630 he was reprimanded by the Dean and Chapter "because he presumed to play verses one (i. e. on) the organ at service tyme, being formerly inhibited by the Dean from doinge the same, by reason of his insufficiency for that solemne service." (*Rimbault, Cheque Book of the Chapel Royal*, 1872, pp. 7, 8, 11, 207.) He is said by Wood (*Ashmole MSS.* 8565, 106, quoted in Rimbault's Cheque Book), to have been Organist of Westminster Abbey, and also that he was one of the Royal Musicians for the lute, but the evidence for both these statements is insufficient. Hawkins (*History of Music*, IV, 65), says that he composed a song of 40 parts which was sung before Charles I. about 1635. The date of his death is unknown. There is a letter from him to his son Philip, dated 1636 in the State Papers (*Calendar, Dom. Series*, CCCIX, 41), and Collier (*History of Dramatic Poetry* (1879) II, 35) quotes warrants of 1641 in which his name occurs as a „Musician for the Waytes" and Gentleman of the Chapel Royal. These documents are not to be found in the calendars of State Papers and it is possible the Thomas Warwick mentioned in them was a son of the organist. Very little of his music has survived, but the odd parts of some anthems are in Add. MSS. 30,478, 30,479, and 29,36-8, and the words of two anthems are in Harl. MS. 6346. Several musicians of the name of Harding occur among the lists of Royal Musicians printed by Nagel (*Annalen der Englischen Hofmusik*, 1895). Edward Harding was a sackbut player in 1625, James Harding was a flute-player from 1581 to 1525, but was dead in February 1626; and another Harding (whose Christian name is not given) was a violinist in 1625. Two Fancies by James Harding occur in Add. MSS. 30,475. Of Galeazzo, Giovanni Pichi, William Oldfield, Jehan Ostermayre, and William Tisdall, nothing is known.

II. THE NOTATION.

In the history of musical notation, there is no more important document than the Fitzwilliam Virginal Book. Transcribed from MSS. of widely different dates and degrees of correctness, by one writer, the pieces, which range from about 1550 to 1620, are so varied in style that almost all the resources of the time, as regards the writing down

Erbin des Richard Candeler aus London, und 2) Elisabeth, Tochter von Francis More aus Sussex. Sir Ferdinando starb am 4. Juni 1618 im Alter von 60 Jahren. Er liegt in der Pfarrkirche von Tottenham, Middlesex, begraben, wo ihm ein Denkmal gesetzt ist, welches sein Bildnis und das seiner ersten Frau, und diejenigen ihrer Eltern trägt. (*Calendars of State Papers, Dom. Ser. Elizabeth and James I. Robinson, History of Tottenham, [1840] II, 42.*) Thomas Warrock, oder Warwick, stammte von einer alten Cumberland'schen Familie ab. Er wurde am 30. Sept. 1586 zum Organisten von Hereford ernannt, welches Amt er nur drei Jahre innehatte. Er heiratete Elisabeth, die Tochter von John Somerville aus Åston Somerville, Gloucester, und wurde durch sie der Vater von Sir Philip Warwick (geb. zu Westminster am 24. Dec. 1609). Im Jahre 1625 folgte er dem Orlando Gibbons als Organist der »*Chapel Royal*«; aber im Jahre 1630 wurde er vom Dekan und Kaplan verwiesen, »weil er sich erlaubte, Verse auf der Orgel während des Gottesdienstes zu spielen, trotzdem dieses ihm früher vom Dekan verboten worden war, da sein Können nicht ausreiche, um dieses während einer so tief-ernsten Feierlichkeit zu thun«. (*Rimbault, Cheque Book of the Chapel Royal 1872*, pp. 7, 8, 11, 207.) Wood sagt (*Ashmole MSS. 8565, 106*, in Rimbaults Cheque-Book citiert), er wäre Organist von Westminster Abbey und einer der königlichen Lautenspieler gewesen; aber die Beweismittel dieser beiden Aussagen sind ungenügend. Hawkins (*History of Music* IV, 65) sagt, er habe ein 40stimmiges Lied geschrieben, welches vor Karl I., etwa 1635 gesungen worden sei. Sein Todesjahr ist nicht festgestellt. Es existiert, unter den »*State Papers*«, ein Brief von ihm an seinen Sohn Philipp, datiert 1636 (*Calendar, Dom. Series CCCIX, 41*), und Collier giebt (*History of Dramatic Poetry (1879) II, 35*) Vollmachtsbriefe aus dem Jahre 1641 an, in denen sein Name als »Musician for the Waytes, and Gentleman of the Chapel Royal« *) vorkommen soll. Diese Dokumente finden sich aber nirgends in den »Calendars of State Papers« vor, und es ist möglich, dass der darin erwähnte Thomas Warwick ein Sohn des Organisten war. Sehr wenige von seinen Kompositionen sind uns erhalten geblieben, aber (einzelne) Stimmen einiger geistlicher Chorgesänge befinden sich in Add. MSS. 30,478. 30,479 und 29,366—368; und die Worte zu zwei geistlichen Chorgesängen sind in Harl. MS. 6346 erhalten. Mehrere Musiker Namens Harding kommen unter den von Nagel gedruckten Verzeichnissen der *Royal Musicians***) (*Annalen der Englischen Hofmusik*, 1895) vor. Edward Harding war ein Posaunenbläser im Jahre 1625, James Harding war ein Flötist von. 1581 bis 1625; war aber im Februar 1626 (schon) tot; noch ein Harding (Vorname unbekannt) war Violinist im Jahre 1625. In Add. MSS. 30,475 kommen zwei Fantasien von James Harding vor. Von Galeazzo, Giovanni Pichi, William Oldfield, Jehan Ostermayre und William Tisdall ist nichts bekannt.

II. DIE NOTENSCHRIFT.

Es giebt in der Geschichte der Musikschrift kein wichtigeres Dokument, als das Fitzwilliam Virginal Book. Von einem Schreiber transcribiert aus MSS. von weit auseinanderliegenden Zeitperioden, und welche betreffs der Genauigkeit bedeutend voneinander abweichen, sind die Stücke, welche

*) Hofkapelle. **) Hofmusiker.

of music, must have been exhausted. The period is a peculiarly interesting one, since it marks the point when the old systems of musical theory, as well as of musical notation, were beginning to give place to those which are now observed, and when the modern laws were only in a very incomplete stage of their development. Many of the difficulties encountered by the writer of the MS. were evidently not reduced to rules, and fairly often we find him trying new experiments in the indication of accidentals, and in other similar points. The regular system of bars with which music has been familiar since the middle of the 17th century, was only in its infancy; still, in general terms it may be said that the use of bars was so clearly a foreshadowing of the present system, that it has not been found necessary to alter the original barring, although in certain cases, dotted bars have been employed to make the difficult passages clearer for the modern musician. The time-signatures present an arrangement that can hardly be made clear without supplementary signs, and accordingly these are among the very few additions made by the editors. Various points connected with the use of accidentals, ornaments, etc. are more fully dealt with below.

THE MODES. The essential difference between the music of the period at which the Virginal Book was written and all that we are accustomed to hear in the present day, lies in the influence which was still exercised by the ecclesiastical modes. The composers of the beginning of the XVIIth century were undoubtedly freeing themselves gradually from the strict modal limitations observed by their predecessors, but they still recognized fully the different characteristics of the ancient scales, and were only dimly conscious of the possibilities opened out by the fusion of the Ionian, Lydian, and Mixolydian modes into our present major scale, and that of the Æolian, Dorian, Phrygian into our present minor. A very large majority of the compositions in the present collection are easily referable to one or other of the modes, and it would be in almost all instances incorrect to speak of them as in such and such a key. In the table of contents of the two volumes the plan has therefore been adopted of adding the number of the mode in cases where there is no distinctive title to the pieces by which they could be identified in other collections. The numbers are those generally recognized as referring to the ecclesiastical modes, and are as follows:

I. Dorian.
II. Hypo-Dorian.
III. Phrygian.
IV. Hypo-Phrygian.
V. Lydian.
VI. Hypo-Lydian.
VII. Mixolydian.

einen Zeitraum von etwa 1550 bis 1620 ausfüllen, so verschieden im Charakter, dass wohl fast alle Mittel der damaligen Zeit, was das Niederschreiben von Musik anbetrifft, erschöpft worden sein müssen. Die Zeitperiode ist auch besonders interessant, insofern als sie die Epoche bezeichnet, in welcher die alten Systeme der Musiktheorie anfingen, denen zu weichen, welche wir jetzt befolgen, und in welcher die Regeln der Jetztzeit noch in einem sehr unvollkommenen Stadium ihrer Entwickelung sich befanden. Viele von den Schwierigkeiten, welche sich dem Schreiber des MS. in den Weg stellten, waren augenscheinlich noch nicht als Regeln festgesetzt, und gar oft merken wir durch, dass er mit Versetzungszeichen und anderen Sachen neue Versuche anstellt. Das regelrechte System der Einteilung in Takte, welches seit Mitte des 17. Jahrhunderts bekannt geworden ist, war noch im Werden begriffen; dennoch kann man im allgemeinen sagen, dass die Anwendung von Taktstrichen eine so deutliche Vorahnung des heutigen Systems war, dass es nicht notwendig erscheint, die alte Takteinteilung zu ändern, wenngleich in gewissen Fällen punktierte Taktstriche angewendet sind, um dem modernen Musiker die schwierigen Passagen zu verdeutlichen. Das System der damaligen Zeitmassangaben lässt sich ohne Zuhilfenahme besonderer Zeichen kaum erklären, und zählen diese dementsprechend zu den wenigen Hinzufügungen, welche die Herausgeber gemacht haben. Verschiedene Punkte, welche sich auf die Anwendung der Versetzungszeichen, Verzierungen etc. beziehen, sind weiter unten vollständiger behandelt.

DIE KIRCHENTÖNE. Der wesentliche Unterschied zwischen der Musik zu der Zeit, in welcher das »*Virginal Book*« geschrieben wurde und der, welche wir heute gewöhnt sind zu hören, ist auf den Einfluss zurückzuführen, welcher noch immer durch die Kirchentöne ausgeübt wird. Die Komponisten aus dem Anfang des 17. Jahrh. befreiten sich zweifellos allmählich von den strengen Beschränkungen, welche ihre Vorgänger beobachteten. Dabei erkannten sie aber im vollen Masse die verschiedenen Charaktere der alten Tonleiter und waren sich dabei nur dunkel der Möglichkeiten bewusst, welche sich ihnen durch die Verschmelzung der ionischen, lydischen und mixolydischen Tonarten mit unserer heutigen Dur-Skala, und die der äolischen, dorischen, phrygischen mit unserer Moll-Tonleiter boten. Bei weitem der grössere Teil der in der Sammlung enthaltenen Kompositionen liesse sich leicht auf eine oder die andere der Kirchentöne zurückführen, und wäre es in fast allen Fällen unrichtig, von denselben zu sagen, dass sie in dieser und jener Tonart geschrieben wären. Aus diesem Grund ist in dem Inhaltsverzeichnis zu den beiden Bänden der Plan überall durchgeführt, dass, wo die Stücke keine besondere, sie in anderen Sammlungen kennzeichnende Benennung tragen, die Nummer des Kirchentons angegeben ist. Die Zahlen sind dieselben, welche allgemein verwendet werden, um die Kirchentöne zu bezeichen, sie lauten:

I. Die dorische,
II. die hypodorische,
III. die phrygische,
IV. die hypo-phrygische,
V. die lydische,
VI. die hypo-lydische,
VII. die mixolydische,

VIII. Hypo-Mixolydian.
IX. Aeolian.
X. Hypo-Æolian.
[XI. and XII. unused modes.]
XIII. Ionian.
XIV. Hypo-Ionian.

Specimens of nearly all these are to be found in the collection, but those most usual are the Dorian, Mixolydian, Æolian, and Ionian, with their plagal counterparts. [The modes indicated by even numbers, and the prefix "Hypo", differ from the "authentic" modes (marked with uneven numbers) mainly in the compass of the melody.] The Phrygian and Lydian occur most rarely. The presence of a flat in the signature does not mean, as it would in the present day, that the key of *F* major or *D* minor is intended; but that the mode, whatever it may be, is transposed a fourth above its normal place. In the table this is indicated by an asterisk after the number of the mode, and the process which is known as "double transposition", (with two flats in the signature) by two asterisks. It is most necessary to bear in mind the modal character of the music in playing compositions in the Mixolydian mode, which seem to be in the key of *G*, but without a sharp in the signature: in these *F* natural is only too easily mistaken for *F* sharp.

VIII. die hypo-mixolydische,
IX. die äolische,
X. die hypo-äolische,
XI und XII. (ungebrauchte Tonarten),
XIII. die ionische,
XIV. die hypo-ionische.

Die Sammlung weist Beispiele von fast sämtlichen Kirchentönen auf, wobei jedoch die dorische, die mixolydische, die äolische und die ionische mit ihren plagalen Gegenbildern am häufigsten vertreten sind. [Die mit geraden Zahlen und der Vorsilbe »Hypo« bezeichneten Kirchentöne weichen von den »authentischen« (mit ungeraden Zahlen versehenen) Tönen im wesentlichen durch den Umfang der Melodie ab.] Am wenigsten häufig kommt der phrygische und der lydische Kirchenton vor. Ein in der Vorzeichnung vorgeschriebenes ♭ bedeutet nicht wie heutzutage, dass die Tonart *F*-dur oder *D*-moll gemeint ist, sondern dass die Tonart, welche sie auch sei, um eine Quarte über ihre normale Stellung transponiert worden ist. In der Tabelle wird dieses durch einen Stern (*) hinter der Zahl des Kirchentons angedeutet; das Verfahren aber, als »doppelte Transponierung« (durch das Voransetzen von zwei ♭♭ in der Vorzeichnung angedeutet) bekannt, wird durch zwei Sterne angedeutet. Es ist von der grössten Wichtigkeit, dass man sich den tonartlichen Charakter der Musik vergegenwärtige, wenn man Kompositionen in dem mixolydischen Tone spielt, welche in der Tonart *G* gedacht, aber ohne das ♯ in der Vorzeichnung erscheinen: in diesen wird nämlich *f*♮ nur zu leicht für *fis* angesehen.

ACCIDENTALS. Closely allied to the modal influence, and indeed due to it in a large degree, is the use of accidentals. In those modes, such as Nos. I, III, VII, and IX with their plagal counterparts, which had no "leading note" a semitone below the tonic or final of the mode, the singers in earlier days were required to introduce accidental notes to supply the want, and without the employment of the written signs which are now in use. The unwritten laws of "musica ficta" must have led to a great amount of confusion when the performers were not fully experienced, and as music became more elaborate, and the instinctive desire for modulation became stronger, written accidentals had to be inserted. But it was long before the rule now in force was established. It seems not to have been absolutely binding that the first flat or sharp in the bar should be so marked, nor was it understood that this first accidental ruled all the notes of the same pitch until the end of the bar, when a new accidental must be introduced. On the one hand, we find many instances of a sharp omitted before the first note to which it obviously refers, and on the other, it is placed before every repetition of the note, even in the same bar. Such passages as the following

are very common. This carelessness, or rather want of system in regard to accidentals, makes many passages ambiguous which would otherwise be perfectly clear; and the editors have been compelled, in many pieces, to supply accidentals which can be only matters of conjecture, and

VERSETZUNGSZEICHEN. Die Anwendung von Versetzungszeichen ist mit den Kirchentönen eng verbunden; ja sie ist sogar gewissermassen wesentlich daraus hervorgegangen. In alten Kirchentönen, wie z. B. in Nr. I, III, VII und IX mit ihren plagalen Gegenbildern, welche keinen Leitton, einen Halbton unter der Tonica oder dem Schluss des alten Kirchentons hatten, mussten die damaligen Sänger Noten mit den hinzugedachten Versetzungszeichen im Geiste ergänzen, und zwar ohne Anwendung der geschriebenen Zeichen, wie wir sie heute gebrauchen. Die ungeschriebenen Regeln der »musica ficta« müssen grosse Konfusion herbeigeführt haben, wenn man es mit unerfahrenen Künstlern zu thun hatte; und als die Musik tiefer durchgeistigte Ausarbeitung erfuhr, und der Drang nach Modulation instinktiv stärker wurde, musste man geschriebene Versetzungszeichen einführen. Es dauerte jedoch eine geraume Zeit, bis die heutige Regel sich festsetzte. Scheinbar wurde nicht verlangt, dass das erste ♯ oder ♭, das im Takte sich geltend machte, angegeben werden musste, noch bezog sich dieses erste Versetzungszeichen auf alle Noten von derselben Tonhöhe, bis zum Schluss des Taktes, wo ein neues Versetzungszeichen gesetzt werden musste. Einerseits finden wir, dass in vielen Fällen ein ♯ vor der ersten Note, auf die es sich jedenfalls bezieht, weggelassen ist; andererseits wird es vor jede Wiederholung dieser Note, sogar in demselben Takte, gesetzt. Solche Passagen oder Stellen, wie die folgende:

sind sehr gewöhnlich. Diese Nachlässigkeit, oder vielmehr dieser Mangel an System mit Bezug auf die Anwendüng der Versetzungszeichen, hat zur Folge, dass viele Stellen, welche sonst

upon which each reader must form his own conclusions. Interpolated accidentals are indicated in all cases by being placed above or below the notes to which they refer, and by being enclosed in brackets.

ganz klar wären, doppeldeutig werden. Die Herausgeber haben daher an vielen Stellen Versetzungszeichen ergänzen müssen, wo sie nur vermutet werden können, und bezüglich welcher jeder Leser für sich urteilen muss. Auf diese Weise eingeführte Versetzungszeichen stehen stets in Klammern und befinden sich über oder unter der Note, auf welche sie sich beziehen.

Sometimes a flat or, more rarely, a sharp, is placed at the beginning of a bar, although the note to which it applies may not be the first of the bar; here it is clear that the accidental governs all the notes of the same pitch in the bar, just as in more modern music.

Manchmal steht ein ♭, oder seltener ein ♯, am Anfang des Taktes, ohne dass die Note, auf die es sich bezieht, die erste im Takte zu sein braucht; in einem solchen Falle ist es klar, dass das Versetzungszeichen allen in dem Takte vorkommenden Noten von derselben Tonhöhe gilt, gerade so wie bei modernerer Musik.

The restoration of a note previously altered by an accidental, by means of a flat or sharp, contradicting a sharp or flat (of course the sign now in use for a natural is of far later origin), is of very rare occurrence; and in the great majority of cases this restoration has been made conjecturally. In dealing with such passages, the character of the mode employed must be borne in mind, and help may often be got by comparing the reading of similar sections, repeated with or without ornamentation. A curious example of the writer's inability to express a progression which was perfectly clear as far as sound is concerned, is to be found in the last bar of vol. ii. p. 270, and the first of p. 271. These stand in the MS.:

Die Wiederherstellung der ursprünglichen Note nach einem Versetzungszeichen vermittelst eines ♭ oder eines ♯, welches ein ♯ oder ein ♭ aufhebt (natürlich ist das Zeichen, das heute als Aufhebungszeichen (♮) gilt, viel späteren Ursprungs), kommt sehr selten vor, und in der grossen Mehrzahl der Fälle ist diese Wiederherstellung nach Mutmassen gemacht worden. In der Behandlung solcher Stellen muss der Charakter des alten Kirchentons berücksichtigt werden und oft wird Klarheit dadurch verschafft, dass man mit anderen ähnlichen Stellen Vergleiche anstellt, welche man dann mit oder ohne Verzierung wiederholt. Ein interessantes Beispiel von des Schreibers Hilflosigkeit in der Aufzeichnung einer Progression, welche Stelle, was sonst den Klang anbetrifft, ganz klar wäre, befindet sich im letzten Takte von Band 2. S. 270, und im ersten Takte auf S. 271. Im MS. lautet sie:

This illustrates the points referred to above, as to the restoration of accidentals. Another instance of a similar kind is in vol. ii. p. 405, where the reading of the MS. is given in the footnote. Brief reference may be made here to the unaccustomed use of accidentals in Bull's "*Ut, re, mi, fa, sol, la*", (vol. i. p. 183); a more detailed discussion of the whole passage will be found at p. XIX.

Dies veranschaulicht die obenerwähnten Punkte bezüglich der Wiederherstellung der Versetzungszeichen. In Band 2 S. 405 kommt ein Beispiel ähnlicher Art vor, wo die Lesart des MS. in einer Textnote angegeben ist. Erwähnt sei noch hier in Kürze die ungewohnte Anwendung von Versetzungszeichen in Bull's »*Ut, re, mi, fa, sol, la*« (Band 1. S. 183); eine eingehendere Besprechung der Stelle befindet sich auf S. XIX.

TIME-SIGNATURES. These have very little to do with the actual value of the contents of the bars, but they indicate rather the ratio of measurement. For the most part they are three in number — the barred semi-circle indicating generally, but not always, all the varieties of quadruple time, whether of eight, four, or two minims' value; the semicircle with a point in it, used for 6—2 and 3—2 time generally (for 3—1 time — *i.e.*, with three semibreves in the bar, the barred semi-circle is used); and thirdly, the figure 3, indicating nearly always 6—4 or 3—4 time, and always followed by the use of black semibreves and black minims, with void notes to indicate what we now call a dotted note of either value. These signatures are of course a survival of the complicated system of Mode, Time, and Prolation, and this use of black notes is practically the last appearance of that system in music.

ZEITMASSANGABEN. Diese haben sehr wenig mit dem wirklichen Werte des Taktinhaltes zu thun; sie deuten vielmehr das Verhältnis der Zählung an. Sie sind grösstenteils drei an der Zahl: erstens der durchstrichene Halbkreis deutet gewöhnlich, doch nicht immer, alle Arten des viertaktigen Zeitmasses an, gleichviel ob der Takt aus acht, vier oder zwei Halbnoten besteht; zweitens der Halbkreis mit einem Punkt darin wird verwendet für 6—2 und 3—2 Takt allgemein (für 3—1 Takt, d. i. wo drei Ganznoten in dem Takte sind, wird der gestrichene Halbkreis gebraucht); und drittens, die Zahl 3, welche fast immer 6—4 oder 3—4 Takt bedeutet, und hierauf folgt immer die Anwendung von schwarzen Ganznoten und schwarzen Halbnoten mit leeren Noten, um anzudeuten, was wir jetzt eine punktierte Note von dem einen oder dem anderen Werte bezeichnen. Diese Vorzeichen sind natürlich ein Überbleibsel des komplizierten Systems von Modus, Tempus und Prolatio, und diese Verwendung der schwarzen Noten ist in Wirklichkeit die letzte Erscheinung jenes Systems in der Musik.

It is evident that the presence of "black minims" and ordinary crotchets in the same bar must lead to confusion, and the translation of these has been often very difficult. A careful comparison of the facsimile, frontispiece to vol. i. with the passage as translated in vol. i. p. 186, will show the principles on which the translation has been made. At the beginning of variation 14, the little "31" [i-e. 3 = 1] opposite the alto part indicates the adoption of triple time, and that the semibreves of the top part are each of them equivalent to three black semibreves in the other. The notes that are apparently crotchets in the latter half of the top line of the facsimile are in reality black minims. The second line exhibits the extraordinary experiment in rhythms that is referred to in the notes. Two ordinary minims in the alto part correspond to three black semibreves in the lowest part, and as soon as the bass changes to two minims, the alto contradicts it by employing three black semibreves. Meanwhile a complicated system of syncopated triple ratios is going on in the tenor part, the result being a problem for the player which no modern composer has ever approached in difficulty. It will be observed that the time-values as between dual and triple ratios is different from that which now prevails. In translating the above and similar passages into modern notation, the division of an ordinary semibreve into three is done by a triplet of minims, just as the equivalent of an ordinary crotchet is three quavers. Here the proportion goes a step further, and the equivalent of a semibreve is a triplet of three black semibreves. The most rapid notes in use are also governed by rules differing from ours, although the practice of the writer is not quite uniform. As a general rule, a group of six notes used as the equivalent of a crotchet (translated here as a sextolet of semiquavers) appears as a sextolet of demisemiquavers, while the eight demisemiquavers which have the same value appear with four strokes to the tails. The difference, which, it will be seen, exactly reverses the procedure with the longer notes, may be best expressed thus:

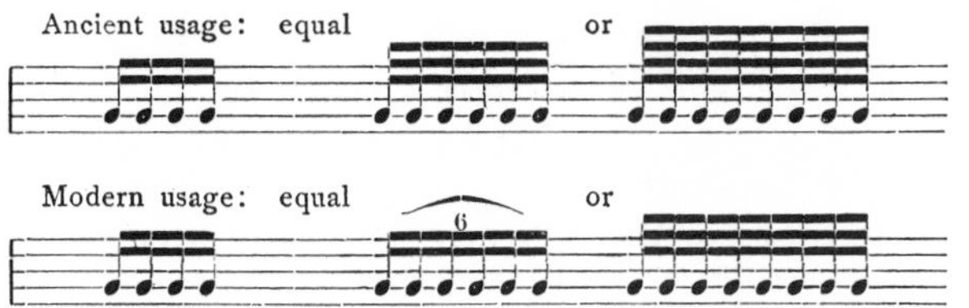

The writer's practice in regard to the grouping of notes will be seen from the facsimiles and the examples given here; in this respect the MS. conforms more closely with modern usage than in any other, for the notes are usually, though by no means always, grouped more or less according to the rhythmical divisions of the bar. In tied notes a little rectangular horizontal stroke is added to the tails of crotchets and minims, as well as the slur by which they are joined as usual. (See frontispiece to vol. i. in the sixth and following bars of the fantasia No. 52. In the same bar, the sixth, the first chord exhibits an arrangement which occasionally is a little confusing. It does not seem to have occurred to the older writers that two notes of the same value could be put upon the same stem, and as there was no room for a separate stem the middle note or notes of a chord are generally unprovided with tails at all. In

Selbstredend musste das Vorkommen von schwarzen Halbnoten und gewöhnlichen Viertelnoten in demselben Takte verwirren, und die Übertragung in's Moderne war oft recht schwierig. Ein sorgfältiger Vergleich der Faksimile (s. Titelblatt zu Bd. 1.) mit der Stelle, wie sie in Bd. 1. S. 186 modernisiert wiedergegeben ist, wird das Prinzip erklären, auf welchem diese Übertragung beruht. Am Anfang der Variation 14 deutet das kleine »31« (d. i. 3 = 1) der Altstimme gegenüber, den Übergang zum ungeraden Zeitmasse an, und dass jede der Ganznoten der Oberstimme gleichwertig ist mit drei schwarzen Ganznoten der anderen. Die Noten, welche in der letzten Hälfte der oberen Linie der Faksimile als Viertelnoten erscheinen, sind in Wirklichkeit schwarze Halbnoten. Die zweite Linie zeigt das interessante Experiment in den Rhythmen, worauf in den Noten verwiesen wird. Zwei gewöhnliche Halbnoten in der Altstimme entsprechen drei schwarzen Ganznoten in der untersten, und, sowie der Bass in zwei Halbnoten übergeht, widerspricht ihm die Altstimme, indem hier drei schwarze Ganznoten verwendet werden. Zugleich spielt sich im Tenor ein kompliziertes System ungerader Zeitmasse ab. Das Ganze stellt dem Spieler ein Problem, dem, was Schwierigkeit anbetrifft, kein moderner Komponist auch nur im entferntesten gleichgekommen wäre. Man wird bemerken, dass das Verhältnis des Dauerwerts zwischen geraden und ungeraden Zeitmassen von dem abweicht, welches heute massgebend ist. In der Übertragung obiger und ähnlicher Stellen in moderne Notenschrift wurde die Zerlegung einer gewöhnlichen Ganznote in drei Teile dadurch erreicht, dass man drei Halbnoten als Triole dafür einsetzte, geradeso wie das Äquivalent einer gewöhnlichen Viertelnote drei Achtelnoten sind. Hier geht das Verhältnis noch einen Schritt weiter und das Äquivalent einer Ganznote ist eine Triole von drei schwarzen Ganznoten. Die kleinwertigsten Noten, die gebraucht wurden, unterliegen Regeln, welche von den heutigen abweichen, jedoch bleibt der Schreiber nicht immer ganz konsequent. Im allgemeinen erscheint eine Gruppe von sechs Noten, welche als Äquivalent einer Viertelnote gilt (hier als Sextole aus Sechzehnteln übertragen) als Sextole aus Zweiunddreissigsteln, während die acht Zweiunddreissigstel, welche denselben Wert haben, mit vier Strichen an den Stielen erscheinen. Der Unterschied, welcher, wie man sieht, den Vorgang mit den längeren Noten umkehrt, lässt sich vielleicht am besten so ausdrücken:

Die Methode, welche der Schreiber mit Bezug auf die Gruppierung der Noten befolgt, ergiebt sich aus den Faksimilen und den hier angeführten Beispielen; in dieser Beziehung gleicht das MS. der modernen Schreibart mehr als in irgend welcher anderen; denn die Noten sind, wenn auch nicht immer, so doch gewöhnlich mehr oder weniger nach den rhythmischen Einteilungen des Taktes gruppiert. Bei gebundenen Noten wird ein kleiner rechteckiger horizontaler Strich den Stielen der Viertel- und der Halbnoten, ausser dem Schleifbogen, durch den sie wie gewöhnlich gebunden werden, angefügt (siehe Titelblatt zu Band 1 im sechsten und in den folgenden Takten

some cases, this leads to ambiguity in regard to their value, for the middle note of these chords may sometimes be taken for a semibreve. In such cases the internal evidence is generally strong enough to leave no doubt of the correct interpretation).

ORNAMENTS. The two ornaments in most common use are and . The first apparently indicates a slide of a third upwards, or a double appoggiatura, and possibly occasionally a mordent; the second seems to be used for a long or short shake, or for either a "Pralltriller" or "Mordent". These signs are so interpreted by Mr. Dannreuther in his Primer of Ornamentation, p. 18. (Novello & Co.) A third sign seems to be employed in very rare instances, figured thus: but it seems probable that the sign is simply a cancelling or correction of the sign wrongly put in. Strong confirmation of the above interpretation of the second sign is afforded by its use in vol. i p. 202 and vol. ii p. 19, where the note so ornamented is approached from a third below.

BARRING. It is necessary, in order to understand the system on which the bars are used in the MS., to remember that the bars are entirely independent of the time-signature. This latter has only to do with the proportional values of the notes to each other; the bars are merely, at this period, a convenient help to the player's eye, and although they usually follow the rhythmic outline of the composition pretty closely, yet they are often very irregular. When a piece begins with long-held notes each bar contains three or four times as much as the bars in the later part of the piece do, when the ornaments are more rapid. An excessive instance of this is seen in vol. ii. p. 353, where the continuous lines, as always, give the barring of the MS., the dotted lines those which are required by modern musicians. As a general rule it seems that the pieces have the longer bars at the beginning rather than at the end.

The writer's use of double bars, or rather of the repeat marks which usually accompany the double bars, is not quite clear. In the first part of the MS. almost every section seems to be marked for repetition, but as the dots are generally omitted in the later pieces, it may be that they are only ornamental. A glance at the elaborate final ornaments in the facsimiles will show that the dots which

der Fantasia Nr. 52). In demselben Takte, dem sechsten, zeigt der erste Accord eine Zusammenstellungsweise, welche zuweilen etwas verwirrt. Es scheint den alten Schreibern nicht eingeleuchtet zu haben, dass man zwei gleichwertige Noten auf einen und denselben Stiel schreiben konnte, und da der Raum für den zweiten Stiel fehlte, so fehlt gewöhnlich der mittleren oder den mittleren Noten der Stiel überhaupt gänzlich. In einigen Fällen führt dies zu Unklarheit bezüglich des Wertes der einzelnen Noten, denn die mittlere Note solcher Accorde wird gar zu leicht mit einer Ganznote verwechselt. In solchen Fällen spricht der Inhalt an sich gewöhnlich genügend, um jeden Zweifel bezüglich der Interpretation zu heben.

VERZIERUNGEN. Die zwei allgemein gebräuchlichsten Verzierungen sind und . Das erstere bezeichnet scheinbar das Gleiten einer Terz nach oben, oder einen Doppelvorschlag, möglicherweise dann und wann auch einen Mordent. Das zweite Zeichen scheint einen langen oder kurzen Triller, oder einen »Pralltriller« oder »Mordent« andeuten zu sollen. So werden diese Zeichen von Herrn Dannreuther in seinem »Primer of Ornamentation p. 18 (Novello & Co.) erläutert. In sehr seltenen Fällen scheint ein drittes Zeichen verwendet worden zu sein, welches so aussieht: ; jedoch darf man vielleicht annehmen, dass dieses Zeichen einfach andeuten soll, dass das fälschlich angegebene Zeichen aufgehoben oder verbessert werden soll. Sehr zu Gunsten dieser Auslegung des zweiten Zeichens spricht die Verwendung, welche es in Band 1 S. 202 und Band 2 S. 19 findet, wo die Annäherung an die so verzierte Note von der unteren Terz aus geschieht.

TAKTEINTEILUNG (durch Taktstriche). Um das System zu verstehen, auf welchem der Gebrauch der Taktstriche im MS. beruht, muss man nicht vergessen, dass die Taktstriche absolut unabhängig sind von dem vorgeschriebenen Zeitmass. Letzteres hat lediglich mit dem relativen Werte der Noten zu einander zu thun; die Taktstriche waren damals lediglich ein Hilfsmittel, um dem Auge des Spielers eine (übersichtliche) Erleichterung zu gewähren; und wenn sie auch der rhythmischen Anlage der Komposition ziemlich getreu folgen, so merkt man doch, dass der Komponist in ihrer Anwendung oft sehr willkürlich verfährt und keiner festen Regel folgt. Wo ein Stück mit langgehaltenen Noten anfängt, enthält jeder Takt drei- bis viermal so viel als die Takte in später folgenden Teilen der Komposition, wo die Verzierungen eine schnellere Ausführung bedingen. Ein Beispiel solchen Übermasses befindet sich im Bd. 2 S. 353, wo die ununterbrochenen Linien, wie immer, die Takteinteilung nach dem MS. angeben, die punktierten Linien dagegen eine solche Takteinteilung, wie sie der heutige Musiker verlangt. Im allgemeinen scheint es Regel zu sein, dass die längeren Takte mehr am Anfange als am Ende stehen.

Des Schreibers Anwendung der Doppelstriche oder der Wiederholungszeichen, welche gewöhnlich mit den Doppelstrichen zusammenhängen, ist nicht ganz klar. Im ersten Teil des MS. scheint fast jeder Abschnitt durch Zeichen zur Wiederholung bestimmt; da jedoch die Punkte in den späteren Stücken fortfallen, sind die Punkte möglicherweise nur zur Zierde. Ein Blick auf die komplizierten Schlussverzie-

occur at every double bar in the earlier portions may be ornamental. They have been retained exactly as they stand in the MS. and the reader must use his discretion as to their interpretation.

DIVISION OF SECTIONS. Closely allied to the double bars is the system of marking off the various sections of the pieces. The simplest arrangement is that employed in sets of variations where the method of numbering is identical with the modern practice. In some of the more elaborate dance-measures and elsewhere the tune itself is in two sections; in this case the latter half, both of the tune and of the variations, is marked with a small figure 2, the larger figures appearing over the first section of each variation. In the case of a piece where each separate section is at once presented in an ornamental shape, the abbreviation "Rep." is used; this seems always to indicate the ornamented version of a simple strain just preceding it. In one composition a double set of ornamental variations occurs, when the second is marked "Rep. 2[a]" (see vol. ii. p. 146,7). The numeration of many of the fantasias in which a rudimentary fugal structure is apparent, follows the successive entries of the theme or answer. In one, No. CCLXI, the numbers are thus indicated up to the twelfth entry, after which the original theme disappears; a marginal note, the words of which have suffered at the binder's hands, contains the words "la fuga ... fuggira" at the point where the numbering leaves off. See note on vol. ii p. 406.

STRUCTURE OF THE INSTRUMENT. A word or two regarding the instrument for which these compositions were written may not be out of place, as it has a close relation to the method in which they should be treated on the pianoforte. The tone of the virginal is identical with that of the spinet or harpsichord, in that the sound of the strings is caused by plucking with quills or tongues of leather. It is a mistake to suppose that because the vibrations were excited in this way they were necessarily evanescent; a fine instrument has very nearly as much power of sustaining a long note as the modern pianoforte, but a perfectly legato passage could not be executed on the older instruments. The effect of rapid runs was exceedingly brilliant and crisp, and fairly rapid repetitions of the same note could be made with good effect, although the modern system of changing the fingers upon the same note is not as successful as repetitions with the same finger. Another peculiarity possessed by many virginals throws light upon a passage which is impossible to play upon the modern pianoforte. At the end of No. LXXII (Philips's arrangement of "Così morirò") occurs, in the left hand, this chord of which the right hand can take no note as it has a full chord of its own above (vol. i p. 287). On many of the instruments in use at this period, the compass of the keyboard is apparently down to *E* only; but as the

rungen in den Faksimiles wird beweisen, dass die Punkte, welche in den älteren Teilen bei jedem Doppelstrich vorkommen, möglicherweise nur zur Ausschmückung dienen. Sie sind genau so wiedergegeben, wie sie im MS. stehen, und muss der Leser bezüglich ihrer Interpretation sich selbst überlassen werden.

EINTEILUNG DER ABSCHNITTE. In enger Verbindung mit den Doppelstrichen steht das System der Einteilung der Stücke nach Abschnitten. Das einfachste System findet in der Aufeinanderfolge von Variationen Verwendung, wo die Numerierungsmethode mit der heutigen identisch ist. Bei einigen der komplizierteren Tanzweisen und auch sonst, zerfällt die Melodie selbst in zwei Abschnitte, wobei die zweite Hälfte der Melodie sowie der Variation mit einer kleinen Zahl 2 bezeichnet wird, während die grösseren Zahlen über dem ersten Abschnitt einer jeden Variation erscheinen. In Fällen, wo bei einem Stücke jeder einzelne Abschnitt gleich in verzierter Form geschrieben ist, steht die Abkürzung »Rep.«; dieses scheint immer die verzierte Version einer demselben direkt vorangehenden einfachen Weise anzudeuten. In einer Komposition kommt eine Doppelfolge von verzierten Variationen vor, von denen die zweite mit »Rep. 2a« bezeichnet ist (siehe Band 2. S. 146, 147). Die Numerierung vieler der Fantasias, welche einen rudimentären fugenartigen Aufbau verraten, richtet sich nach der folgerechten Wiederkehr des Themas oder der Antwort. In einer Fantasia Nr. CCLXI sind die Zahlen so angegeben bis zum zwölften Eintritt (des Themas), worauf das ursprüngliche Thema verschwindet; eine Randbemerkung, die unter des Buchbinders Händen gelitten hat, enthält die Worte: »la fuga . . . fuggira«, ebenda, wo die Numerierung aufhört. Siehe Anmerkung Band 2. S. 406.

KONSTRUKTION DES INSTRUMENTS. Einige Worte über das Instrument, für welches diese Kompositionen geschrieben wurden, dürften hier wohl am Platze sein, da es in naher Beziehung zu der Methode steht, in welcher sie auf dem Klavier behandelt werden sollten. Der Ton des Virginal ist identisch mit dem des Spinetts oder des Cembalo, insofern als der Klang der Saiten durch Rupfen mittels (Feder-) Kielen oder Lederläppchen erzeugt wird. Es wäre grundfalsch, wenn man schliessen wollte, dass die so erzeugten Vibrationen notwendigerweise nur von kurzer Dauer sein müssten; ein gutes Instrument hält eine lange Note beinahe ebenso lange an wie unser modernes Klavier; dagegen konnte man eine absolute Legatopassage auf den älteren Instrumenten nicht ausführen. Der Effekt schneller Läufer war ein ausserordentlich brillanter und abgerundeter; es war auch möglich, mit gutem Effekt einen Ton ziemlich schnell repetieren zu lassen, obgleich die heutige Methode, die Finger auf derselben Note zu wechseln, nicht so guten Erfolg erzielt, als das Repetieren mit demselben Finger. Eine weitere Eigentümlichkeit, welche viele Virginale besassen, wirft ein Licht auf eine Passage, welche sich unmöglich auf dem modernen Klavier spielen liesse. Am Schluss von Nr. LXXII (Philips Arrangement von »Cosí moriró« kommt in der linken Hand folgender Akkord vor, von welchem die rechte Hand keine Note spielen kann, da sie oben selbst einen

lowest *F* sharp and *G* sharp were most rarely required, the triads of which these are basses being most seldom used, the keys representing these notes in the ordinary arrangement were adapted to the strings giving the lowest *D* and *E*, while the bottom note of the instrument (apparently *E*) was tuned to *C*. The arrangement of the seven lowest notes of the instrument was as follows:

Apparent notes: *E*, *F*, *F* sharp, *G*, *G* sharp, *A*, *B* flat.
Real sounds: *C*, *F*, *D*, *G*, *E*, *A*, *B* flat.

It follows therefore, that the chord occuring at the end of No. LXXII, was quite easily played on a virginal tuned with this "short octave" arrangement, for the keys played would be those represented in the present day thus:

Even more important is the question of the system on which the instruments were tuned. It is always taken for granted that keyed instruments of all classes were tuned in just intonation, in such a way that while the key nearly related to *C* major were more or less exactly in tune, those keys which are represented by a great number of sharps or flats were execrably discordant. In just intonation, there is no doubt that the disagreeable effect of what are called "false relations" was far less than it is in our ears; and whatever may be the explanation, every student of old music knows that the composers of the period showed an extraordinary indifference to the juxtaposition of adjacent semitones, although they would have been repelled by many chords which now-a-days please the most fastidious musicians. In certain conventional passages, such as this very common cadence —

one can still trace a beauty which one would not sacrifice by either flattening the upper part or sharpening the lower. To this pattern many passages conform in the book, a rapid figure of greater elaboration representing the lower part of these two and running counter to the leading note of the other part at every turn. Yet there are many other cases where the leading note is left out, as if by carelessness, where it is obviously needed as much by the nature of the mode in which the piece is cast as by the requirements of modern ears. Modern ears, to say the truth, cannot be absolutely trusted in these matters; there are numerous instances of false relations that simply cannot be altered without doing despite to the general design of the piece in which they occur, for a sharp added here will necessitate another somewhere farther on, and before long we shall be

vollen Akkord zu greifen hat (Band I. S. 287). Viele Instrumente aus der damaligen Periode hatten einen Spielumfang, welcher, wie es scheint, abwärts nur bis zum *E* ging; da aber das tiefste *fis* und *gis* höchst selten benutzt wurden, da die Dreiklänge, zu welchen diese Noten den Bass bilden, äusserst selten angewendet wurden, so waren die Tasten, welche diese Noten nach der gewöhnlichen Vorrichtung repräsentierten, nach den Saiten eingerichtet, indem sie das tiefste *D* und *E* angaben, während die tiefste Note des Instruments (augenscheinlich *E*) auf *C* gestimmt wurde. Das Arrangement der sieben tiefsten Noten des Instruments war folgendes:

Dem Auge scheinbare Noten: *E*, *F*, *Fis*, *G*, *Gis*, *A*, *B*.
Wirkliche Töne: *C*, *F*, *D*, *G*, *E*, *A*, *B*.

Hieraus geht hervor, dass der am Schlusse von Nr. LXXII sich befindliche Akkord auf einem nach dieser »kurzen Oktave« gestimmten *Virginal*, sich ganz leicht spielen liess, denn die angeschlagenen Tasten würden heute so geschrieben stehen:

Noch wichtiger sogar aber ist die Frage, nach was für einem System die Instrumente gestimmt wurden. Es wird immer als selbstverständlich angenommen, dass Tasteninstrumente aller Arten nach absolut reiner Intonation gestimmt wurden, nämlich so, dass während die Tonarten welche *Cdur* am nächsten oder nahe verwandt sind, mehr oder weniger genau gestimmt wurden; diejenigen, welche eine grosse Anzahl von ♯♯ oder ♭♭ verlangten, aber abscheulich verstimmt waren. Bei absolut reiner Stimmung unterliegt es keinem Zweifel, dass sogenannte »Querstände« dem Ohre bei weitem nicht so unangenehm klangen wie es bei unserer heutigen Stimmung des Klaviers der Fall ist; und was auch die Erklärung dieser Wahrnehmung sein mag, es weiss es jeder in der alten Musik Erfahrene, dass die damaligen Komponisten eine ausserordentliche Gleichgültigkeit gegen die Nebeneinanderstellung von Halbtönen verrieten, während manche Akkorde, welche heutzutage den verwöhntesten Musikern gefallen, den Alten abstossend klingen würden. In gewissen altherkömmlichen Passagen, wie z. B. in folgender sehr gewöhnlichen Kadenz:

empfindet das Ohr noch immer einen Reiz, den man nicht gern dadurch opfern möchte, dass man die obere Stimme erniedrigte, oder die untere erhöhte. Nach diesem Muster richten sich viele Passagen in dem Buche; eine schnell zu spielende kompliziertere Figur in der unteren Stimme in Gegenbewegung zum Leitton der anderen Stimme begegnet uns immer wieder. Trotzdem kommen viele andere Fälle vor, in denen der Leitton, scheinbar durch Nachlässigkeit, ausgelassen ist, wo sowohl der Kirchenton, in dem das Stück geschrieben ist, sowie das Ohr des heutigen Musikers, ihn unbedingt verlangen darf. Dem modernen Ohre darf man bei solchen Sachen jedoch, wenn man wahr sein will, nicht absolutes Vertrauen schenken; es giebt unzählige Beispiele von Querständen, welche sich nicht abändern lassen, wenn man die ganze Anlage des Stückes, in welchem sie vorkommen, nicht ausser Acht lassen will; denn fügt man hier

led into a far worse plight than if we had left the original passage alone.

But if we take it for granted that just intonation was the almost universal rule, it is not less clear that some method, possibly a very rough and ready one, of obtaining something like temperament was in use at the time of date of this MS.

In the extraordinary "*Ut*, *re*, *mi*, *fa*, *sol*, *la*" of Bull, already referred to more than once in this introduction, the principle of a circle of keys is fully recognized, for the successive entries of the theme proceed by rising a whole tone each time, strict conformity to this plan would, it is evident, bring back the original entry on *G* at the seventh step, but in order to complete the number of the twelve semitone, Bull goes from *F* (entry 6), to *A* flat, by rising a tone and a half. If this can ever have been endurable to educated ears some system of compromise must have been in practice, and the fact that Zarlino, before 1588, had advocated the adoption of a division of the octave into twelve equal semitones, for lutes and keyed instruments, suggests that his system may have been put into practice in England, at a date long before the universal adoption of the modern method of tempering the scale (see vol. i p. 184). The first bar of the bottom line of p. 183 shows the difficulty caused by the absence of any method of expressing enharmonic equivalents. As the fourth entrance of the subject is to consist of a hexachord beginning on *D* flat, the first note has to be expressed as *D* flat, in spite of the circumstance that this note makes its appearance as *C* sharp, the mediant in the triad of *A* major. The passage is of such importance in the history of notation that the writer's makeshift way of expressing himself has been left unaltered. Any player who can attempt the rhythmic problem further on may be trusted to read this passage correctly.

ein ♯ hinzu, so verlangt eine weitere Stelle wieder ein ♯, und ehe wir uns versehen, ist die Verlegenheit, in der wir uns befinden, eine viel grössere, als wenn wir die Stelle hätten stehen lassen, wie sie ursprünglich geschrieben war.

Nehmen wir es aber als zugegeben an, dass genaue Stimmung die fast allgemein vorherrschende Regel war, so liegt es nichtsdestoweniger klar auf der Hand, dass irgend eine möglicherweise sehr primitive Methode zur Entstehungszeit dieses MS. verwendet wurde, welche so etwas wie Temperierung ermöglichte.

In der merkwürdigen Komposition »*Ut*, *re*, *mi*, *fa*, *sol*, *la*«, von Bull, auf die mehr als einmal in der Einleitung schon Bezug genommen wurde, wird das Prinzip eines wiederkehrenden Kreises von Tonarten völlig anerkannt, denn die folgerechte, wiederholte Wiederkehr des Themas geschieht jedesmal um einen Ganzton erhöht, was, streng durchgeführt, naturgemäss den ursprünglichen Eintritt (des Themas) auf *G* bei der siebenten Stufe herbeiführen würde. Um aber die Zahl der zwölf Halbtöne voll zu machen, geht Bull von *F* (beim sechsten Eintritt [des Themas]) auf *As* über, indem er anderthalb Ton erhöht. Wenn (musikalisch) gebildete Ohren dieses haben ertragen können, so muss irgend ein Ausgleichsystem vorhanden gewesen sein, und die Thatsache, dass Zarlino schon vor dem Jahre 1588 dazu riet, dass man für die Lauten und Tasteninstrumente eine Einteilung der Oktave in zwölf gleiche Halbtöne einführen sollte, — macht es wahrscheinlich, dass sein System lange vor der allgemeinen Einführung der heutigen Temperierung der Skala (siehe Bd. 1. S. 184) in England angewendet worden sein muss. Der erste Takt der untersten Linie auf Seite 183 zeigt, welche Schwierigkeit der Mangel an irgend einer Methode, enharmonische Äquivalente auszudrücken, erzeugte. Da der vierte Eintritt aus einem Hexachord auf *Des* beginnend, bestehen soll, so muss die erste Note als *Des* bezeichnet werden, trotzdem diese Note als *Cis*, die Terz des Dreiklangs *A* dur, erscheint. Diese Stelle ist von so grosser Wichtigkeit in der Geschichte der Notenschrift, dass wir des Schreibers notbehelfliche Art, sich auszudrücken ungeändert gelassen haben. Von dem Spieler, welcher sich an das weiterhin folgende rhythmische Problem wagt, darf man erwarten, dass er diese Stelle richtig lesen wird.

CONTENTS OF VOL. I.

Note. The Roman numbers in square brackets refer to the modes. See Introduction, p. XII.

INHALT VON BAND I.

Anmerkung. Die Römischen Zahlen in viereckigen Klammern beziehen sich auf die Tonarten. Siehe Einleitung S. XII.

*) From this point the numbering of the pieces ceases in the MS. — Von hieran hört das Numerieren der Stücke im MS. auf.

NOTES*) TO VOLUME I.

Vol. I, p. 1. Chappell, p. 121. In Ward's list. This set of variations appears to be a continuation of Byrd's set of 22 variations (see i. 267). Ward says, "This tune was first composed by William Byrde with twenty-two variations; and afterwards thirty others were added to it by Dr. Bull." Another copy is in Cosyns, p. 139.

P. 12. The beginning of variation 20 gives a good instance of the notation of triplets. In the first bar the crotchets of the alto part are marked "61" and the same sign is used apparently with reference to both alto and bass parts at the beginning of the next bar, although the proportional division of the triplets is changed.

P. 17. The beginning of variation 28 is marked with a cross, and the numbers 1, 2, 3, are placed beneath the first three bars, as indicating that the hands must be crossed during these three.

P. 19. In bar 2, notice the rare occurrence of indications of fingering.

P. 27. A copy of this Pavana, with its accompaniyng Galliard, is in Add. MS. 30,485, fol. 75b.

P. 42. See p. 153, where the same set of variations, with slight alterations, is attributed to John Munday. A comparison of the two versions of the same work is instructive as regards the addition of accidentals in the text. The great majority of the accidentals conjecturally added in No. IX are found in the text of No. XLII, and vice versa. No. XLII has besides a final variation of some importance. Chappell,

*) LIST OF BOOKS REFERRED TO IN THE NOTES.

Add. MSS. Additional Manuscripts in the British Museum, London.

Chappell. "The Ballad Literature and Popular Music of the Olden Time; a History of the Ancient Songs, Ballads, and the Dance Times of England, with numerous Anecdotes and entire Ballads. Also a Short Account of the Minstrels. By W. Chappell, F. S. A. The whole of the Airs harmonized by G. A. Macfarren." (No date.)

Cosyns. Benjamin Cosyns' Virginal Book, a MS. volume in Her Majesty's Library at Buckingham Palace.

Forster. Will. Forster's Virginal Book, another MS. volume in the Buckingham Palace Library, dated 1624.

Nevell. My Lady Nevell's Booke, a MS. collection of Virginal music in the possession of the Marquess of Abergavenny, copied by J. Baldwine of Windsor in 1591.

Ward. Lives of the Gresham Professors, by John Ward (1740), containing a list of Virginal Compositions by Dr. John Bull, who was the first Gresham Professor of Music, from 1596 to 1607.

ANMERKUNGEN*) ZU BAND I.

Band I, S. 1. Chappell, S. 121. In Wards Verzeichnis. Diese Folge von Variationen scheint eine Fortsetzung von Byrd's Folge von 22 Variationen zu sein (cf. 1. 267). Ward sagt: »Diese Melodie wurde zuerst von William Byrd mit zwei und zwanzig Variationen komponiert; später kamen dreissig weitere von Dr. Bull dazu.« Eine andere Abschrift findet sich in Cosyns, S. 139 vor.

S. 12. Der Anfang von Variation 20 ist ein gutes Beispiel von der Niederschrift der Triolen. Im ersten Takte sind die Viertelnoten der Alt-Stimme mit »61« bezeichnet, und dasselbe Zeichen wird scheinbar für Alt- und Bass-Stimme am Anfang des nächsten Takts gebraucht, obgleich die Einteilung der Triolen in ihrem Verhältnis zu einander geändert ist.

S. 17. Der Anfang von Variation 28 ist mit einem Kreuz (nicht ♯) versehen, und die Zahlen 1, 2, 3 stehen unter den ersten drei Takten, andeutend, dass die Hände während sie diese drei Takte spielen, sich kreuzen sollen.

S. 19. Hier ist, was sonst eigentlich selten vorkommt, der Fingersatz angegeben, und ist bemerkenswert.

S. 27. In Add. MS. 30,485, fol. 75b steht eine Abschrift dieser Pavane, mit der sie begleitenden Galliarde.

S. 42. Siehe S. 153, wo dieselbe Folge von Variationen mit unbedeutenden Abänderungen dem John Munday zugeschrieben wird. Eine Vergleichung der beiden Versionen desselben Werkes ist lehrreich bezüglich der Hinzufügung von Versetzungszeichen im Texte. Die grosse Mehrzahl der in Nr. IX nach Gutdünken hinzugefügten Versetzungszeichen befindet sich in dem Text zu No. XLII und umgekehrt.

*) VERZEICHNIS DER IN DEN ANMERKUNGEN ERWÄHNTEN BÜCHER.

Add. MSS. Additional Manuscripts im British Museum, London.

Chappell. Balladen-Litteratur und Volkslieder aus alter Zeit; Geschichte der alten Lieder, Balladen und Tanzweisen Englands, mit zahlreichen Anekdoten und vollständigen Balladen. Dazu ein kurzer Aufsatz über die Fahrenden Sänger. Von W. Chappell, F. S. A., = Mitglied des Künstler-Vereins. Sämtliche Arien oder Melodien von G. A. Macfarren harmonisiert. (Ohne Datum.)

Cosyns. Benjamin Cosyns' Virginal-Buch; ein M. S.-Band in Ihrer Majestät Bibliothek im Buckingham-Palast.

Forster. Will. Forster's Virginal-Book; noch ein M.S.-Band in der Bibliothek im Buckingham Palast. Datum 1624.

Nevell. Lady Nevells Buch, eine Sammlung von »Virginal«-Kompositionen im M. S., im Besitz des Marquess von Abergavenny, abgeschrieben von J. Baldwine aus Windsor, i. J. 1591.

Ward. Biographien der Gresham-Professoren von John Ward (1740), enthält ein Verzeichnis von Virginal-Kompositionen von Dr. John Bull, dem ersten Gresham-Professor der Musik, von 1596 bis 1607.

pp. 140, 142: Another setting by Byrd is in Cosyns, p. 157, and Forster, p. 324, and a third for lute by Francis Pilkington, Mus. Bac. is in Add. MS. 31,392, fol. 26b.

P. 47. Chappell, pp. 122, 147, 218, 660, 771.

P. 54. This galliard is intended to follow Lord Lumley's Pavan, p. 149. It is mentioned in Ward's List. A copy is in B. Cosyns, p. 120.

P. 57. Chappell, p. 149.

P. 62. In Ward's List.

P. 66. This tune appears as "Bony sweet Robin", arranged by Farnaby, vol. ii. p. 67.

P. 67 line 3, last bar. The sign **:S:** occurs here in the same position in the MS., where the passage so noted begins a line.

P. 70. In Ward's List.

P. 72. Chappell, pp. 240, 775. See vol ii. p. 94 where the tune is arranged by Thomas Tomkins.

P. 74. Another setting of this tune, by Giles Farnaby, is given in vol. ii. p. 481, and a similar tune is called "The Chirping of the Lark" in Wooldridge's edition of Chappell's "Old English Popular Music", Vol. i. p. 177.

P. 81. It was wrongly assumed, at the time this part was issued, that "El. Kiderminster" was the author of the piece. It is merely inscribed with that name, the space at the end of the piece, where the author's name usually occurs, being left blank.

P. 83. The authorship of this prelude is established by its occurrence in *Parthenia* where it is ascribed to Byrd.

P. 87. "Ho-Hoane" is evidently a corruption for "Och-one", the Irish lament. See Chappell, p. 793.

P. 89. The triplets and sextolets in the last two lines are indicated exactly in the modern fashion in the MS. by way of exception to the general rule.

P. 99. Chappell, p. 104. See also Add. MSS. 29,485, fol. 18b; 30,485, fol. 17b; 31,392, fol. 20; and Forster, pp. 96 (a setting by Morley) and 202. Also see vol. ii. p. 103 ff. for a setting by Byrd of this pavan and galliard. This and the next seven pieces are in Ward's list.

P. 105. The change of time, indicated here by [$\frac{6}{4}$], appears in the MS. as a figure 3 between the two staves.

P. 107. This variation to the Quadran Pavan appears as "The Quadran Pavan" in Cosyns, p. 94.

P. 124. This pavan and the following galliard are among the most carefully fingered pieces in the collection. Notice that the left-hand fingering reverses the order of the right; thus No. 1 in the lower stave indicates the little finger of the left hand, no. 5 the left thumb. The contraction "Dor." appears below the title in the MS. It cannot refer to the Dorian mode (see note on vol. ii. p. 23). No. XLVIII, p. 177, is apparently another galliard to the same pavan.

Nr. XLII hat ausserdem noch eine Schluss-Variation von nicht geringer Bedeutung. Chappell, SS. 140, 142: Eine andere Bearbeitung von Byrd steht in Cosyns S. 157 und Forster S. 324; eine dritte für die Laute von Francis Pilkington, Mus. Bac. kommt vor in Add. MS. 31,392, fol. 26b.

S. 47. Chappell, S. 122, 147, 218, 660, 771.

S. 54. Diese Galliarde soll folgen auf Lord Lumleys Pavane, S. 149. Sie ist in Wards Verzeichnis erwähnt. Eine Abschrift steht in B. Cosyns, S. 120.

S. 57. Chappell, S. 149.

S. 62. In Ward's Verzeichnis.

S. 66. Diese Melodie kommt in Band II, S. 77 als »Bony sweet Robin«, arrangiert von Farnaby, vor.

S. 67. Reihe 3, letzter Takt. Das Zeichen **:S:** kommt hier in derselben Stellung im MS. vor, wo die so bezeichnete Stelle eine Reihe anfängt.

S. 70. In Ward's Verzeichnis.

S. 72. Chappell, SS. 240, 775. Siehe Band II, S. 94, wo die Melodie von Thomas Tomkins arrangiert ist.

S. 74. Eine andere Bearbeitung dieser Melodie, von Giles Farnaby, steht in Band II, S. 481 angegeben; und eine ähnliche Melodie, betitelt »The Chirping of the Lark« befindet sich in Wooldridges Ausgabe von Chappells »Altenglische Volksmusik«, Band I, S. 177.

S. 81. Als dieser Teil erschien, wurde fälschlicherweise angenommen, dass »El. Kiderminster« der Verfasser des Stückes sei. Es trägt einfach diesen Namen; während der Raum, wo gewöhnlich des Verfassers Name steht, freigelassen ist.

S. 83. Die Autorschaft dieses Prelude ist dadurch festgestellt, dass sie in Parthenia vorkommt, wo sie dem Byrd zugeschrieben wird.

S. 87. »Ho-Hoane« ist jedenfalls eine Korrumpierung von »Och-one«, des Iren Klage. Siehe Chappell, S. 793.

S. 89. Die Triolen und Sextolen in den letzten beiden Reihen sind, abweichend von der allgemeinen Regel, im MS. genau so angegeben wie in moderner Musik.

S. 99. Chappell, S. 104. Siehe auch Add. MSS. 29,485, fol. 18b; 30,485, fol. 17b; 31,392, fol. 20; und Forster, SS. 96 (eine Bearbeitung von Morley) und 202. Siehe auch Band II, S. 103 ff., wo diese Pavana und Galliarde von Byrd bearbeitet vorkommen. Dieses Stück und die folgenden sieben stehen in Ward's Verzeichnis.

S. 105. Der Wechsel im Zeitmass, hier durch [$\frac{6}{4}$] angedeutet, erscheint im MS. als eine Zahl 3 zwischen den beiden Notensystemen.

S. 107. Diese Variation zu der Quadran Pavane erscheint als »The Quadran Pavane« in Cosyns, S. 94.

S. 124. Diese Pavane und die darauf folgende Galliarde gehören zu den Stücken der Sammlung, welche am sorgfältigsten mit Fingersatz versehen sind. Beachtenswert ist, dass der Fingersatz für die linke Hand eine Umkehrung des sonst in der rechten Hand beobachteten bewirkt; so z. B. bedeutet Nr. 1 in dem unteren Notensystem den kleinen Finger der linken Hand, Nr. 5 den linken Daumen. Die Abkürzung »Dor.« erscheint unterhalb des Titels im MS. Sie kann sich nicht auf die dorische Tonart beziehen (siehe Anmerkung zu Bd. II, S. 23). Nr. XLVIII, S. 177 ist scheinbar eine andere Galliarde zu derselben Pavane.

P. 131. This piece, under the title of "Galiardo Saint Thomas Wake" is given in *Parthenia*, after a "Pavan Saint Thomas Wake" founded on the same tune.

P. 138. Called in Ward's list "Fantasia upon a Plain Song".

P. 141. The figure 1 refers to the numeration of Farnaby's pieces.

P. 144. The authority for assigning this to Gibbons is given in the foot-note to this page. A setting by Byrd of the same tune is on p. 263 of this volume.

P. 149. In the MS. there is the note "Vide the Galliard to this Paven, p. 27". The Galliard is on p. 54 of this volume.

P. 153. See note on p. 42 above.

P. 158. In Ward's list this prelude is called "Praeludium to Gloria tibi Trinitas". The similarity of the themes will be noticed.

P. 160. In Ward's List.

P. 162. The complicated cross-rhythms in lines 2 and 3 are very carefully indicated in the MS. where each triplet is preceded by "61" or "32", sometimes by both together, and each pair of even crotchets by the sign "₵".

P. 163. In Ward's list. There are two similarly-named compositions by Bull in Add. MSS. 23,623, fol. 169, and 31,403, p. 14 respectively, but all three are different.

P. 170. In Ward's List.

P. 177. See above, note to p. 124. The contraction "Dor." appears below the title.

P. 181. Two other pieces by Blitheman with the same title and upon the same plain-song are in Add. MSS. 31,403 fol. 8b and 9 and 30,485 fol. 58b.

P. 183. In Ward's List. On the curious enharmonic change, mentioned in the foot-note, see introduction p. XIX.

P. 186. On the cross-rhythms in variation 15, see Introduction, p. XV. The frontispiece to this volume, represents a page of the MS. beginning at line 3, bar 2 of this page, and going down to p. 189, bar 1.

P. 196. The figure "2" continues the numbering of Farnaby's compositions through the volume. The last piece numbered is vol. ii. 360. See Chappell, p. 60.

P. 202. This duet is not written in score in the MS., but the part for the first virginal is written by itself, above that for the second.

P. 203. This pavan and the following galliard also occur in Nevell, fol. 92, and Forster, p. 217. It is worth noting that both here and in Peter Philips's setting of the pair of pieces with the same title, the word "Passamezzo" in each case precedes the work "Pavan" and follows the word "Galiard".

P. 213. First line, second bar, the first note in the bass should be *D*, not *F*.

P. 214. This piece has often been printed. Copies of it are in Nevell, fol. 149, in Add. MSS. 31,403 fol. 25b and 30,485 fol. 65 and in Forster, p. 130. See Chappell, pp. 137—140, 428.

S. 131. Dieses Stück, betitelt »Galiardo Saint Thomas Wake«, kommt in Parthenia vor und steht direkt hinter einer "Pavan Saint Thomas Wake", welche dieselbe Melodie zur Grundlage hat.

S. 138. In Ward's Verzeichnis lautet der Titel »Fantasia über einen Cantus firmus«.

S. 141. Die Zahl 1 bezieht sich auf die Numerierung von Farnabys Stücken.

S. 144. Die Autorität, gestützt auf welche dieses Stück dem Gibbons zugeschrieben wird, ist in der Textnote dieser Seite angeführt. Eine Bearbeitung von Byrd derselben Melodie steht auf S. 263 dieses Bandes.

S. 149. Im MS. befindet sich die Anmerkung: »Vide the Galliard to this Paven. p. 27«. Die Galliarde steht auf S. 54 dieses Bandes.

S. 153. Siehe die Anmerkung auf S. 42, oben.

S. 158. In Ward's Verzeichnis heisst dieses Prelude: »Praeludium zu Gloria tibi Trinitas«. Die Ähnlichkeit der Themata ist auffällig.

S. 160. In Ward's Verzeichnis.

S. 162. Die schwierigen Wechsel-Rhythmen in den Reihen 2 und 3 sind im MS. sehr genau bezeichnet: vor jeder Triole steht »61« oder »32« oder beide Zahlen, und vor jedem Paar gerader Viertelnoten steht das Zeichen »₵«.

S. 163. In Ward's Verzeichnis. Zwei ähnlich betitelte Kompositionen von Bull stehen in den Add. MSS., eine in Nr. 23,623, fol. 169, die andere in Nr. 31,403, S. 14; aber alle drei sind verschieden.

S. 170. In Ward's Verzeichnis.

S. 177. Siehe obige Anmerkung zu S. 124. Die Abkürzung »Dor.« steht unterhalb des Titels.

S. 181. In Add. MSS. 31,403, fol. 8b und 9, und 30,485, fol. 58b befinden sich zwei weitere Stücke von Blitheman mit demselben Titel und über denselben Cantus firmus.

S. 183. In Ward's Verzeichnis. Siehe Einleitung S. XIX, bezüglich des interessanten enharmonischen Wechsels, der in der Textnote erwähnt wird.

S. 186. Siehe Einleitung S. XV bezüglich der Wechselrhythmen in Variation 15. Das Titelblatt zu diesem Bande ist eine Reproduktion einer Seite des MS. und fängt mit Reihe 3, Takt 2 dieser Seite an, und geht bis S. 189, Takt 1.

S. 196. Die Zahl »2« setzt die Numerierung von Farnabys Kompositionen durch den ganzen Band fort. Das letztnumerierte Stück steht in Band II, S. 360. Siehe Chappell, S. 60.

S. 202. Dieses Duett ist im MS. nicht in Partitur geschrieben, die erste Virginalstimme ist für sich geschrieben und steht über der zweiten Virginalstimme.

S. 203. Diese Pavane und die folgende Galliarde kommen auch in Nevell, fol. 92, und in Forster, S. 217 vor. Es ist bemerkenswert, dass das Wort »Passamezzo« hier sowie in Peter Philips' Bearbeitung der beiden Stücke mit demselben Titel in beiden Fällen dem Worte »Pavan« vorangeht, dem Worte »Galiard« folgt.

S. 213. Erste Reihe, zweiter Takt: die erste Note im Bass sollte D, nicht F sein.

S. 214. Dieses Stück ist öfters gedruckt worden. Abschriften davon kommen vor in Nevell, fol. 149; in Add. MSS. 31,403, fol. 25b und 30,485, fol. 65, und in Forster, S. 130. Siehe Chappell, SS. 137—140, 428.

P. 216. Line 3, the first notes in the right hand should be *D*, *F*, not *B*, *D*.

P. 217. The top line, left hand, the melody of the last half-bar stands in the MS. a third too high; the right reading is shown by the little sign or "direct" at the foot of the page in the MS.

P. 218. Chappell, pp. 53, 60—62, 196; a copy also in Nevell. fol. 46. Another setting by Byrd is in vol. ii. p. 430.

P. 226. As this piece is called "Hughe Ashtons grownde", in Nevell. fol. 153b, the abbreviation "Treg." probably does not indicate authorship.

P. 229. Bottom line, first bar, left hand. The bass chords of the next bar appear simultaneously with those of this bar in the MS.

P. 234. A copy of this in Forster, p. 244. A different setting is in Nevell, fol. 173b, of which a copy is also in Forster, p. 366. The abbreviation "Rep." line 3, occurs here for the first time in the MS. See Introduction, p. XVII. Here as often elsewhere it seems to indicate the ornamented version of a strain just preceding it; thus it is the equivalent of the phrase used by Bach, Couperin, and Bach, and others, "Les agrémens de la même sarabande".

P. 238. The beginning of line 4, right hand stands thus in the MS.:

and it is possible it should be read thus, the "32" being a time-direction, and the last two notes being semiquavers by mistake:

P. 240. The minim in the tenor part, at the beginning of line 4, is not in the MS., but is indicated by a "direct"; showing that it was to have been put into the right hand stave, to allow the left to take the bass note, *G*.

P. 248. See Chappell, p. 69, where the melody is printed in Byrd's arrangement. A copy is in Nevell, fol. 166b.

P. 254. See Chappell, p. 162.

P. 258. See Chappell, p. 209.

P. 260. The figure in lines 4 and 5, consisting of a group of four demi-semiquavers followed by a sextolet of semiquavers, represents a group of ten demi-semiquavers in the MS. This solution of the measurement accords best with the general character of the variation.

P. 263. See p. 144. Copies of this setting are in Nevell, fol. 109 Add. MSS. 30,485, p. 67 (dated 1590) and 31,403, fol. 23b. See also Forster, p. 118.

P. 267. See p. 1 .and note. Other copies of this setting are in Nevell, fol. 135, Forster, p. 74.

P. 280. This and the two following pieces are transcriptions of a madrigal in three sections, by Luca Marenzio.

S. 216. Reihe 3: die ersten Noten in der rechten Hand müssten D, F., nicht H, D sein.

S. 217. Die oberste Reihe, linke Hand: die Melodie des letzten Halbtaktes steht im MS. eine Terz zu hoch; die korrekte Lesart wird durch das kleine Zeichen oder den »Custos« unten im MS. angedeutet.

S. 218. Chappell, SS. 53, 60—62, 196; eine Abschrift steht auch in Nevell, fol. 46. Eine andere Bearbeitung von Byrd steht in Bd. II, S. 430.

S. 226. Da dieses Stück in Nevell, fol. 153b »Hughe Ashton's grownde« betitelt ist, so deutet die Abkürzung »Treg« wohl nicht auf die Autorschaft.

S. 229. Unterste Reihe, erster Takt, linke Hand. Die Bass-Accorde des nächsten Takts erscheinen im MS. gleichzeitig mit denen dieses Takts.

S. 234. Eine Abschrift dieses Stücks in Forster, S. 244. Eine andere Bearbeitung steht in Nevell, fol. 173b, wovon wieder eine Kopie auch in Forster, S. 366 vorkommt. Die Abkürzung »Rep.«, Reihe 3, kommt hier zum erstenmale im MS. vor. Siehe Einleitung, S. XVII. Hier, und oft an anderen Stellen, scheint es die verzierte Version einer ihm direkt vorausgehenden Weise anzudeuten; also wäre es gleichbedeutend mit dem Vermerk von Couperin, Bach und anderen «Les agrémens de la même sarabande».

S. 238. Der Anfang von Reihe 4, rechte Hand, steht so im MS.:

möglicherweise sollte diese Stelle folgendermassen gelesen werden, indem »32« als Zeitmassangabe anzusehen wäre, die beiden letzten Noten aus Versehen als Sechzehntelnoten angegeben:

S. 240. Die Halbnote im Tenor am Anfang von Reihe 4 steht nicht im MS., ist aber durch ein Leitzeichen (Custos) angedeutet, wodurch dem Spieler zu verstehen gegeben wird, dass die Halbnote in das Notensystem der rechten Hand gesetzt werden sollte, damit die linke die Bassnote *G* greifen konnte.

S. 248. Siehe Chappell, S. 69, wo die Melodie mit Byrd's Bearbeitung gedruckt ist. Eine Abschrift befindet sich in Nevell, fol. 166b.

S. 254. Siehe Chappell, S. 162.

S. 258. Siehe Chappell, S. 209.

S. 260. Die Figur in Reihen 4 und 5 aus einer Gruppe von vier Zweiunddreissigstelnoten bestehend und von einer Sextole von Sechzehntelnoten gefolgt, repräsentiert im MS. eine Gruppe von zehn Zweiunddreissigstelnoten. Diese Lesart der Einteilung stimmt am besten mit dem allgemeinen Charakter der Variation überein.

S. 263. Siehe S. 144. Abschriften dieser Bearbeitung stehen in Nevell, fol. 109; Add. MSS. 30,485, S. 67 (dat. 1590) und 31,403, fol. 23b. Siehe auch Forster, S. 118.

S. 267. Siehe S. 1 und Anmerkung. Andere Abschriften dieser Bearbeitung befinden sich in Nevell, fol. 135 und Forster, S. 74.

S. 280. Dieses und die beiden nächsten Stücke sind Transkriptionen einer Madrigale in drei Abschnitten von

The numbers below the titles refer to this continuous series of Philips's arrangements and compositions, and end with No. LXXXVIII.

P. 288. The original form of this piece, a six-part madrigal, has not been found.

P. 299. See note on p. 203.

P. 321. The name may possibly indicate that the theme of the pavan is by Tregian. The second word of the title should of course be "Dolorosa", and the words "Set by" should be omitted, as they do not occur in the MS.

P. 329. "Julio" (or rather Giulio) "Romano", was the name by which Caccini was generally known; the song is in his "Nuove Musiche", and is his best known composition.

P. 332. The correct title of the original composition is "Margot labourez vos vignes".

P. 335. A Fantasia on the same subject, by Byrd, is in vol. ii. p. 406.

P. 351. The rhythmic structure of this little piece can only be understood by taking the first half of each bar (in the first section only) as in 6—4 time, the latter half as in 3—2. In the second section the latter rhythm remains unchanged.

P. 367. The abbreviation "Ph. Tr." appears in the MS.

P. 373. This absurd piece of music, by an Italian composer otherwise unknown, completes the first part of the MS. The remainder of the page on which it ends (p. 176), is left blank, and four pages after it are empty. When the music is resumed, the numbering of the pieces is discontinued. This cessation of the numbering is here indicated by enclosing the numbers in square brackets.

P. 378. Sweelinck's first appearance in the collection is noted by the figure 1 below the title.

P. 384. The two contributions of Thomas Warrock are duly numbered 1 and 2 respectively.

P. 394. The actual reference in the MS. is to "pag. 94"; the number 188 refers to the present volume.

P. 411. See Chappell, p. 110. A copy is in Nevell, fol. 142b.

P. 415. Tregian's authorship is assumed on what is perhaps rather slender evidence; it is clear that the writer cannot have acquired much skill of composition.

P. 423. Given in Ward's list.

P. 427. This piece, the oldest dated composition in the collection, is one of four settings of plain-songs similarly named, by Tallis. In Add. MS. 30,485 fol. 26 a collection of Virginal Music headed "Extracts from Lady Nevil's Music Book", but containing much besides, is a "Felix namque" by Tallis, against which (in a later hand), is written "1562" in the Virginal Book, but it is a different composition from either this or the following and a fourth occurs in Add. MS. 31,403, fol. 27b. The long-held note near the end indicates quite clearly that the piece was intended for the organ, and there is little doubt that the whole class of settings of plain-songs were primarily meant for the church.

Luca Marenzio. Die Zahlen unter den Titeln beziehen sich auf diese ununterbrochene Serie von Philips' Bearbeitungen und Kompositionen und schliessen mit Nr. LXXXVIII.

S. 288. Die ursprüngliche Form dieses Stückes, eine sechsstimmige Madrigale, ist nicht aufgefunden worden.

S. 299. Siehe Anmerkung zu S. 203.

S. 321. Möglicherweise deutet der Name an, dass das Thema der Pavane von Tregian herrührt. Das zweite Wort des Titels sollte natürlich »Dolorosa« heissen, und die Worte »Set by« (arrangiert von) müssten fortfallen, da sie im MS. nicht stehen.

S. 329. »Julio« (oder vielmehr Giulio) »Romano« war der Name, unter welchem Caccini gewöhnlich bekannt war; das Lied ist in seinen »Nuove Musiche« enthalten, und ist diejenige von ihm, die am meisten bekannt ist.

S. 332. Der richtige Titel der ursprünglichen Komposition lautet »Margot labourez vos vignes«.

S. 335. Eine Phantasie über dasselbe, von Byrd, steht in Bd. II, S. 406.

S. 351. Der rhythmische Aufbau dieses kleinen Stückes wird erst dann klar, wenn man die erste Hälfte eines jeden Taktes (d. h. nur im ersten Abschnitt) so auffasst, als ob sie in 6—4 Takt, die letzte Hälfte in 3—2 Takt geschrieben wäre. Im zweiten Abschnitte bleibt der letztere Rhythmus ungeändert.

S. 367. Die Abkürzung »Ph. Tr.« kommt im MS. vor.

S. 373. Dieses absurde Musikstück, von einem sonst unbekannten Komponisten, vollendet den ersten Teil des MS. Der Rest der Seite, auf welcher derselbe endigt (S. 176), ist freigelassen mitsamt vier darauf folgenden Seiten. Wo die Musik wieder anfängt, hört die Numerierung der Stücke auf, welches Aufhören hier dadurch angedeutet wird, dass die Zahlen in viereckige Klammern gesetzt sind.

S. 378. Sweelincks erstes Erscheinen in der Sammlung wird durch die Zahl 1 unter dem Titel vermerkt.

S. 384. Die zwei Beigaben von Thomas Warrock sind, die eine mit der Zahl 1, die andere mit 2 numeriert.

S. 394. In Wirklichkeit bezieht sich das MS. auf »pag. 94«; die Zahl 188 hat Bezug auf den vorliegenden Band.

S. 411. Siehe Chappell, S. 110. Eine Abschrift steht in Nevell, fol. 142b.

S. 415. Die Annahme, dass Tregian der Verfasser wäre, beruht auf vielleicht etwas schwachem Zeugnis; man sieht deutlich, dass der Schreiber kein sehr geschickter Komponist gewesen sein kann.

S. 423. Steht in Ward's Verzeichnis.

S. 427. Dieses Stück, welches die älteste Datierung von allen in der Sammlung enthaltenen Kompositionen aufweist, ist eine von vier Bearbeitungen ähnlich betitelter Canti fermi von Tallis. In Add. MS. 30,485, fol. 26, einer Sammlung von Virginal-Musik, überschrieben »Extracts from Lady Nevil's Music Book«, die aber vieles andere enthält, steht ein »Felix namque« von Tallis, bei welcher (von einer späteren Hand) die Jahreszahl »1562« in das Virginal Book geschrieben ist; aber diese Komposition weicht gänzlich ab sowohl von dieser wie von der folgenden; eine vierte steht in Add. MS. 31,403, fol. 27b. Die lang angehaltene Note, die beinahe am Schlusse steht, zeigt deutlich, dass das Stück für die Orgel geschrieben war, und unterliegt es kaum einem Zweifel, dass sämtliche Bearbeitungen der Canti fermi ursprünglich dafür bestimmt waren, in der Kirche gespielt zu werden.

I.
Walsingham.

JOHN BULL.

3.

4.

5.

6.
(♮)
(♯)
7.

8.

9.

*) Semiquavers in M S.
Sechzehntel in der Handschrift.

(♮)
(♯)
(♯)
(♯)
10.

* G in M. S.
G in der Handschrift.

** F sharp in M. S.
Fis in der Handschrift.

13.

14.
15.

16.

17.

*Quavers in M. S.
Achtel in der Handschrift.

** Crotchet in M. S.
Viertelnote in der Handschrift.

20.
3
3
3
(♮)
(♮)
(♯)
21.
3

*) Semiquavers in M S.
Sechzehntel in der Handschrift.

23.
(3)
24.

(♯)
(♯)
(♯)(♯)
3
25.

26.
(♯)
(♯)
(♯)
(♯)
(♯)
27.

28.

Doctor
JHON BULL.

II.
Fantasia.

JOHN MUNDAY.

JHON MUNDAY.

III.
Fantasia.

JOHN MUNDAY.

*C in M. S.
C in der Handschrift.

* Quavers in the M.S.
Achtel in der Handschrift.

Faire Wether.
Lightning.
Thunder.
Faire Wether.

* C in M.S.
C in der Handschrift.

IV.
Pavana.

FERDINANDO RICHARDSON.

3.
FERDINANDO RICHARDSON.

V.
Variatio.

FERDINANDO RICHARDSON.

* The notes from * to * are a third lower in the M. S.
Die Noten von * bis * stehen eine Terz tiefer in der Handschrift.

2.
6

3.
6
6
(♮)
(♭)
(♯)
FERDINANDO RICHARDSON.

VI.
Galiarda.

FERDINANDO RICHARDSON.

*Semiquavers in M S.
Sechzehntel in der Handschrift.

VII.
Variation.

FERDINANDO RICHARDSON.

2.
3.

FERDINANDO RICHARDSON.

VIII.
Fantasia.

WILLIAM BYRD.

(♮)
(♯)
(♮)
(♮)
6
6

4
3
4
1
2

WILLIAM BYRD.

IX.
Goe from my window.*

THOMAS MORLEY.

2.

* See no. XLII. where the same piece, with slight variations, is attributed to John Munday.
Vergleiche Nr. XLII, wo dasselbe Stück, mit geringen Veränderungen, John Munday zugeschrieben wird.

3.
4.

3 4
5
(♮)
(♯)
(♯)

6.

* sic. The sharp is possibly a clerical error, as it does not occur in the corresponding place in no. XLII.
sic Das Kreuz ist möglicherweise ein Schreibfehler, da es an der entsprechenden Stelle in Nr. XLII nicht vorkommt.

X.
Jhon come kisse me now.

WILLIAM BYRD.

2.

(♯)

(♯)

3.

4.
5.
(♯)
6.

7.
(♯)
(♯)
8.
(♯)

9.
10.

11.
(♮)
(♯)
12.
3
13.

14.

WILLIAM BYRD.

XI.
Galliarda to my L.[ord] Lumley's Paven.

(See Nº XLI.)

JOHN BULL.

* Quavers in the M.S.
Achtel in der Handschrift.

(♯)
(♯)
(♯)
(♯)
DOCTOR BULL.

XII.
Nancie.

THOMAS MORLEY.

2.

* A in M.S.
A in der Handschrift.

6
3.
6

In this piece the sextolets of semiquavers appear in the M.S. as demisemiquavers ; and the groups of 8 demisemiquavers as semi-demisemiquavers

In diesem Stück erscheinen die Sextolen der 16tel Noten im Manuscript als 32tel ; und die Gruppen von acht 32tel als 64tel

XIII.
Pavana.

JOHN BULL.

(♯)

(♯)

(♯)

(♯)

(♯)

*

(♯)

* The M. S. has A D.
A D in der Handschrift.

2.

(♯)
DOCTOR BULL.

XIV.
Alman.

ANON.

* G in M. S.
G in der Handschrift.

XV.
Robin.

JOHN MUNDAY.

* The sign **:S:** occurs here in the same position in the MS.
Das Zeichen **:S:** kommt hier in derselben Stellung im MS. vor,

XVI.

Pavana.

M. S.

* Quavers in M. S.
Achtel in der Handschrift.

XVII.
Galiarda.

JOHN BULL.

* E in the M. S.
E in der Handschrift.

XVIII.
Barafostus' Dreame.

ANON.

2.

3.

* E in the MS.
E in der Handschrift.

* G in the M.S.
G in der Handschrift.

XIX.
Muscadin.

ANON.

XX.
Alman.

ANON.

2.
L.H.

XXI.
Galiarda.

ANONYMOUS.

* Semiquavers in the M. S.
Sechzehntel in der Handschrift.

These 6 notes are semiquavers in the M. S.
Diese 6 Noten sind Sechzehntel in der Handschrift.

XXII.
Præludium.

ANON.

XXIII.

Præludium.

"EL. KIDERMINSTER."

XXIV.
Prælludium.

[WILLIAM BYRD.]

* This bar is altered from the M. S., which gives 21 demisemiquavers in the left hand.
Dieser Takt, welcher in der Handschrift für die linke Hand 21 Zweiunddreissigstel enthält, ist hier geändert worden.

4
5

XXV.
Præludium.

ANON.

* A F in M. S.
A F in der Handschrift.

** This bar is added conjecturally; something has evidently been omitted between pp. 41 and 42 of the M. S., and the "directs" at the end of p. 41 indicate the notes here given at the beginning of the added bar, not those of the next following bar.

Dieser Takt ist nach Vermuthung hinzugefügt worden; augenscheinlich ist zwischen den Seiten 41 und 42 der Handschrift etwas ausgelassen, denn die Anführungszeichen am Ende der Seite 41 zeigen die Noten an, welche hier den Anfang des hinzugefügten Taktes bilden, nicht diejenigen des nächstfolgenden Takts.

XXVI.
The Irishe Ho-Hoane.

ANON.

XXVII.
Pavane.

F. RICHARDSON.

* Semiquavers in M.S.
Sechzehntel in der Handschrift.

(♯)
2.
(♯)
(♮)

3.
(♮)
6
FERDINANDO RICHARDSON.

XXVIII.
Variatio.

F. RICHARDSON.

* In the M. S. B flat in the signature appears at the second line, [bar 5] and continues throughout the piece.

In der Handschrift erscheint ein ♭ in der Vorzeichnung in der zweiten Linie, [Takt 5] und wird von da an im ganzen Stück beibehalten.

2.

FERDINANDO
RICHARDSON.

XXIX.
Galiarda.

F. RICHARDSON.

* The M. S. gives the middle note of this chord as C, which is clearly a mistake for D.
Die Handschrift giebt die mittlere Note dieses Accords als C an, welches offenbar falsch ist und D sein soll.

3.

FERDINANDO RICHARDSON.

XXX.
Variatio.

(♮)

(♯)

**

(♭)

*Quavers in M. S. / Achtel in der Handschrift.

**Semiquavers in M. S. / Sechzehntel in der Handschrift.

2.
(♭)
(♮)

*C in M.S.
C in der Handschrift.

(♮)
(♭)
Ferdinando Richardson.

XXXI.
The Quadran Pavan.

JOHN BULL.

(#)

(#)

(#)

(#)

2.

(♯)
(♯)
(♮)
(♯)
(♮)
3.
(♮)
(♯)
(♯)

4.

5.

6.

* A third higher in the M.S.
Ein Terz höher in der Handschrift.

** D in M.S.
D in der Handschrift

*** A in M.S.
A in der Handschrift.

**** C in M.S.
C in der Handschrift.

****** Semiquavers in the M.S.
Sechzehntel in der Handschrift.

7.

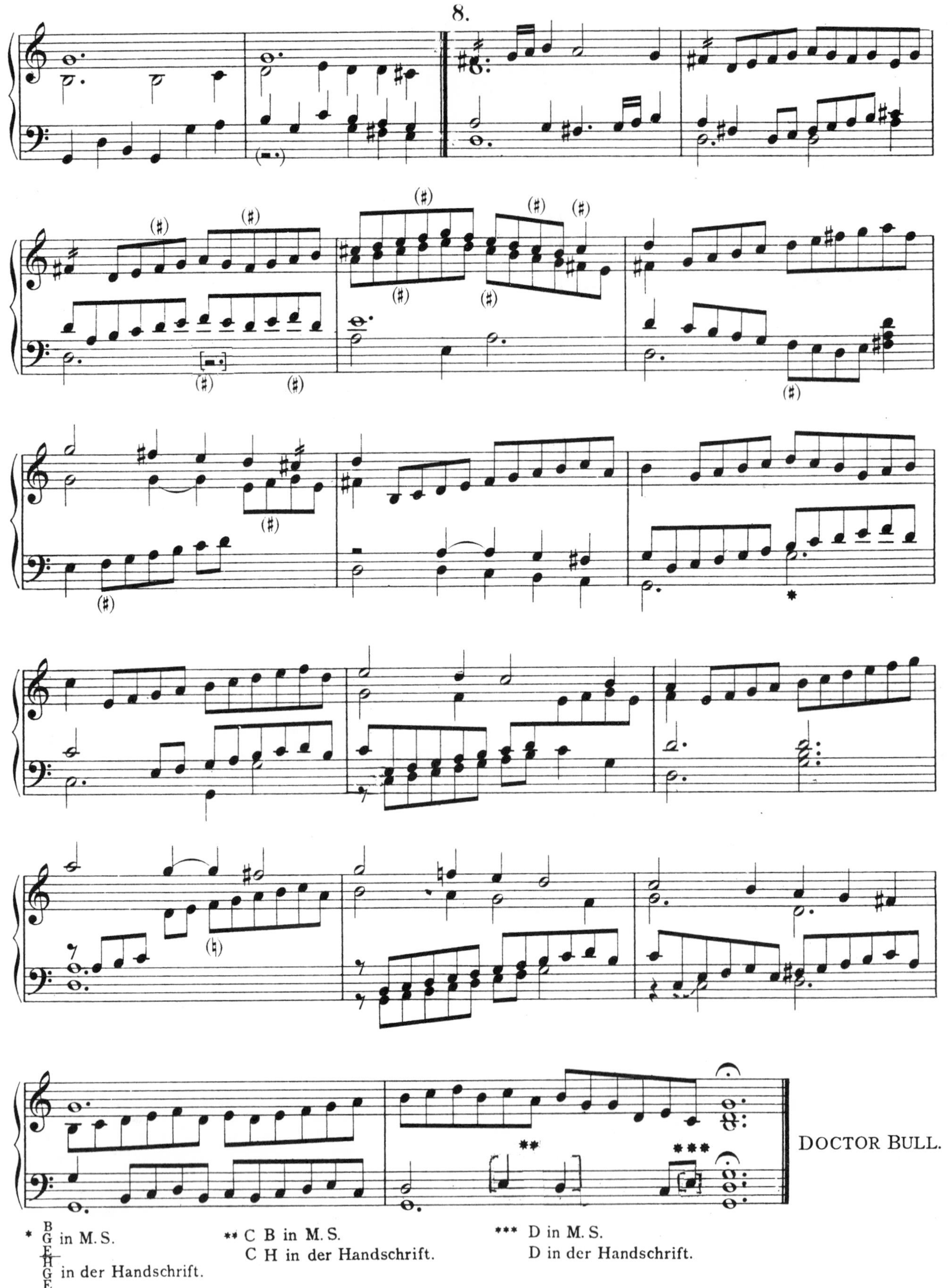

* B G E in M.S.
H G E in der Handschrift.

** C B in M.S.
C H in der Handschrift.

*** D in M.S.
D in der Handschrift.

XXXII.

Variation of the Quadran Pavan.

JOHN BULL.

(#)

2.

(♮)

(♮)

(♮)

3.

(♯)
4.
(♯)
(♯)
(♯)
(♮)
(♯)

* Semiquaver in M S.
Sechzehntel in der Handschrift.

6.

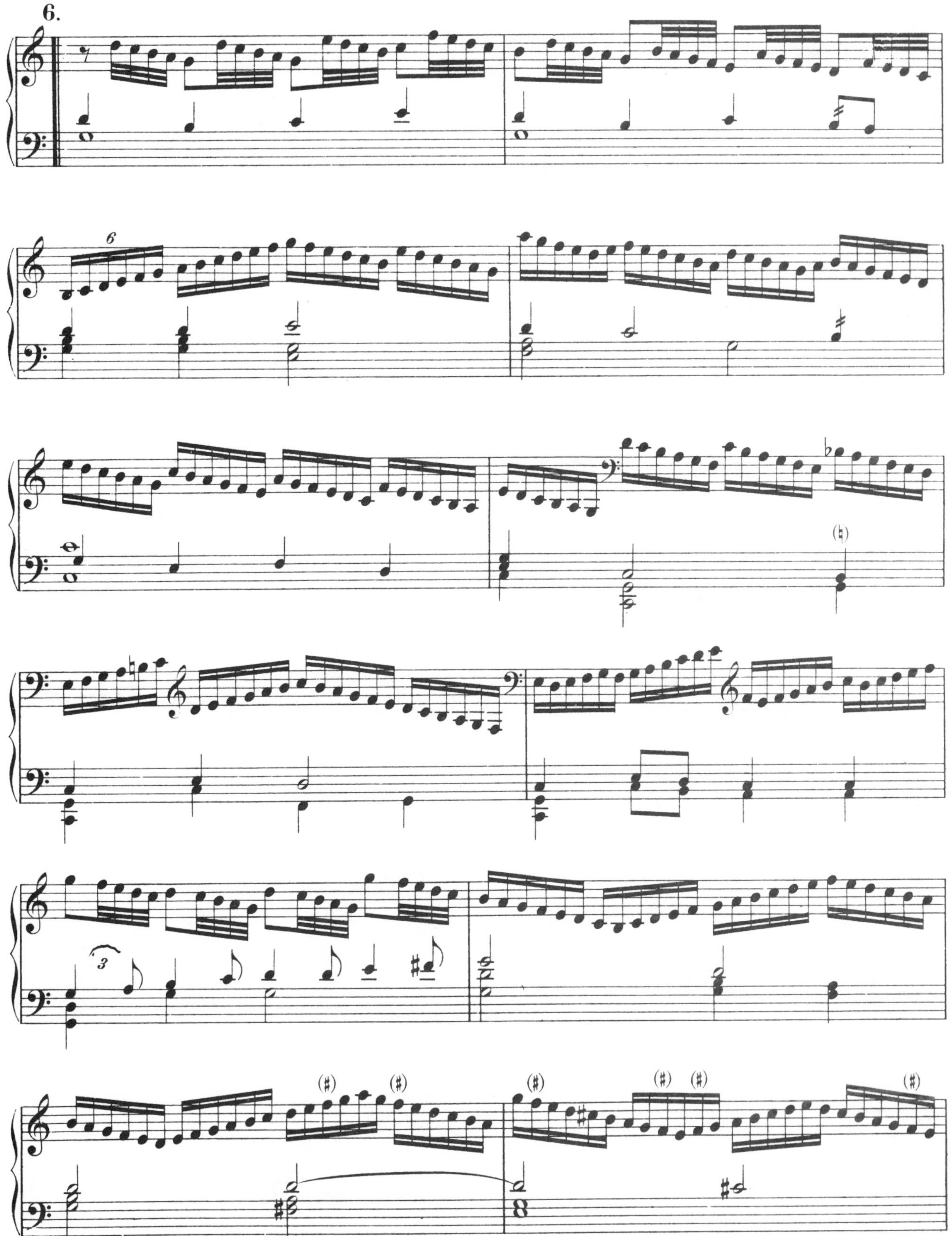

* In the M. S. the Bass of this and the following two bars is written a third lower.
Im M. S. ist der Bass dieses und der nächsten beiden Takte eine Terz tiefer geschrieben.

7.

*) F in the M.S.
F in der Handschrift.

XXXIII.
Galiard to the Quadran Pavan.

JOHN BULL.

(♯)

(♯)

(♯)

2.

(♯)

(♯)

3.
4.
5.

(♮)
(♭)
(♮)
6.

7.
8.

9.

10.

11.
(♯)
(♯)
(♯)
(♯)

12.
(♮)
(♯)
DOCTOR BULL.

XXXIV.
Pavana.

JOHN BULL.

* C in M. S.
C in der Handschrift.

* A cross is inserted in the M. S. at this place, and a marginal note added, "L. M."; it is not clear what is referred to.
Hier ist im Manuskript ein Kreuz und eine Randnote „L. M." beigefügt; es ist nicht klar, worauf sich dies bezieht.

* The flats in these two bars are supplied conjecturally; the presence of a sharp, here represented by a natural, implies the B flats preceding it.
Die ♭ in diesen zwei Takten sind nach Vermuthung ergänzt; aus dem Vorkommen des ♮ ist zu schliessen, dass vor den vorhergehenden Noten h immer ♭ zu lesen ist.

* G sharp in the M S.
Gis in der Handschrift

** The second half of this bar, and the parallel passages two and four bars later appear in the M. S. as a quaver followed by 6 demisemiquavers.
Die zweite Hälfte dieses Taktes und die Parallelstellen dazu 2 und 4 Takte später bestehen im Manuskript aus einem Achtel und 6 Zweiunddreissigsteln.

XXXV.
Galiard to the Pavan.

JOHN BULL.

* The F in the alto part is sharp in the M. S. but the passage seems to require a natural.
Das F in der Altstimme ist in der Handschrift Fis. Doch scheint der Zusammenhang F zu verlangen.

** A in the M. S.
A in der Handschrift.

3.
DOCTOR BULL.

XXXVI.
Saint Thomas Wake.

JOHN BULL.

3.
(♯)

4.

5.
DOCTOR BULL.

XXXVII.
In Nomine.

DOCTOR BULL.

* A in M. S.
A in der Handschrift.

* G in the M.S.
G in der Handschrift.

XXXVIII.

JOHN BULL.

(♯)
(♯)(♮)
(♯)
(♯)
(♯)
(♯)
DOCTOR BULL.

XXXIX.
Pavana.
1.

ROBERT JOHNSON, SET BY GILES FARNABY.

* C in the MS.
C in der Handschrift.

2.

3.

ROB. JHONSON. SETT BY GILES FARNABIE.

XL.
The woods so wilde.*

ORLANDO GIBBONS.

(♭) (♮) (♭)

2. **

* The piece breaks off, after the first two bars of section 5, a the rest of the page being left blank; the latter part of the composition is here supplied, from a copy in the British Museum, (Add. MSS. 31,403, fol. 21–23.) It is there ascribed to Orlando Gibbons, and in the early sections several very slight differences exist between the two MSS. mostly in the matter of ornaments.
Das Stück bricht hinter den ersten zwei Takten der 5. Section ab, der Rest des Blattes ist weiss gelassen.
Der Schluss der Composition ist hier nach einer Handschrift im British Museum (Add. MSS. 31,403, fol. 21-23) ergänzt. Dort wird sie dem Orlando Gibbons zugeschrieben; im ersten Theil der Sectionen finden sich einige ganz geringfügige Abweichungen zwischen beiden Handschriften, namentlich in Bezug auf die Verzierungen.

** Quavers in M.S.
Achtel in der Handschrift.

(♯)
(♮)
(♯)
(♯)
3.
4.

5.
Add. MS. 31, 403 fol. 21-23.

* The MS has a natural to the B.
Die Handschrift hat vor dem B ein Auflösungszeichen.

Mr. Orlando Gibbons.

XLI.
Pavana of my L[ord] Lumley.

JOHN BULL.

(#)

* F in the MS.
F in der Handschrift.

(#)
(♮)
3
3.

DOCTOR BULL.
Vide the Galliard to this Paven p. 54.
vgl. Seite 54.

XLII.

Goe from my window.*

JOHN MUNDAY.

* This is virtually the same composition as Nº 9, which is attributed to Morley, variation 8 is peculiar to this version.

Dies ist völlig dieselbe Composition wie Nº 9, die dem Morley zugeschrieben wird; die 8te Variation ist dieser Fassung eigenthümlich.

3.
4.

* C sharp in MS.
Cis in der Handschrift.

** The bar within brackets is added from Nº 9.
Der eingeklammerte Takt ist aus Nº 9 ergänzt.

*** F in MS.
F in der Handschrift.

7

* C in M S.
C in der Handschrift.

XLIII.
Præludium.

DOCTOR BULL.

DOCTOR BULL.

*) C in the M.S.
C in der Handschrift.

XLIV.
Gloria tibi trinitas.

DOCTOR BULL.

* A sharp appears before this G, evidently anticipating that belonging to the next note.
Vor diesem G steht ein Kreuz, offenbar statt vor der folgenden Note.

XLV.
Salvator mundi.

DOCTOR BULL.

2.

3.

* In the manuscript written a third too low.
Im Manuscript eine Terz zu tief geschrieben.

* A in M.S.
A in der Handschrift.

** F in M.S.
F in der Handschrift.

XLVI.
Galliarda.

DOCTOR BULL.

(#)

(#)

2.

(#)

(♮)(♮)

*The 3 bars from ✲ to ✲ are evidently incorrect in the M.S. They stand thus:
Die 3 Takte von ✲ bis ✲ sind in der Handschrift augenscheinlich falsch. Sie lauten so:

(♯)
3.
DOCTOR BULL.

XLVII.
Variatio.

JOHN BULL.

(♯)
(♮)
2.
(♯)

3.

DOCTOR BULL.

XLVIII.
Galiarda
to the PAVEN No XXXIV.

JOHN BULL.

3.

DOCTOR BULL.

XLIX.
Præludium.

THOMAS OLDFIELD.

* Semiquaver in M. S.
Sechzehntel in der Handschrift.

L.
In Nomine.

WILLIAM BLITHEMAN.

WILLIAM BLITHMAN.

LI.
Ut, re, mi, fa, sol, la.

JOHN BULL.

* This interesting experiment in enharmonic modulation is thus tentatively expressed in the M.S.; the passage proves that some kind of "equal temperament" must have been employed at this date.

Dieser interessante Versuch einer enharmonischen Verwechselung ist im Manuscript so niedergeschrieben; die Stelle beweist, dass offenbar schon damals eine Art von „gleichschwebender Temperatur" angewandt wurde.

5
(♭)
(♭)
(♭)
6
(♭)
(♭)
7
(♭)
(♭)

* In the manuscript written a third too low.
Im Manuscript sind eine Terz zu tief geschrieben.

* Minim in M.S.
Halbe Note in der Handschrift.

* Minim in M. S.
Halbe Note in der Handschrift.

LII.
Fantasia.

WILLIAM BYRD.

3
3

* Crotchet in M. S.
Viertelnote in der Handschrift.

* F in MS.
F in der Handschrift.

9
4
9
4
2
4.
2
(♯)

6
WILLIAM BYRD.

LIII.
The K[ing's] Hunt.
2.

GILES FARNABY.

GILES FARNABIE.

LIV.
Spagnioletta.
3.

GILES FARNABY.

2.

GILES FARNABIE.

* A in M.S.
A in der Handschrift.

LV.
For Two Virginals.
4.

GILES FARNABY.

LVI.
Passamezzo Pavana.

WILLIAM BYRD.

* F in M. S.
F in der Handschrift.

12
4

4.
(6)
(♯)
(3)
(3)
(3)
(♭)
(♯)
(♯)
(♯)
(♯)

5.
(♭)
(♮)
(♭)
(♯)
6.

* B D in the M. S.
H D in der Handschrift.

LVII.
Galiardas Passamezzo.

WILLIAM BYRD.

3.
(♯) (♯) (♯)(♮)(♯)

4.
5.

* Minim in M. S.
Halbe Note in der Handschrift.

LVIII.
The Carmans Whistle.

WILLIAM BYRD.

* D in M.S.
D♭ in der Handschrift.

6.
7.

* The notes from * to * are a third higher in the M.S.
Die Noten von * bis * stehen in der Handschrift eine Terz höher.

LIX.
The Hunt's up.

WILLIAM BYRD.

* Crotchet rest in M.S.
Viertelpause in der Handschrift.

* C in the MS.
C in der Handschrift.

7.

8.

9.
(♭)
(♭)
(♭)

10.
11.

* G in M.S.
G in der Handschrift.

LX.
Treg [ian's] Ground.

WILLIAM BYRD.

* These two notes, required to complete the bar, are supplied from the figure in the second bar of section 4.
Diese beiden Noten, die zur Vollständigkeit des Taktes erforderlich sind, werden nach der Figur im zweiten Takt des 4ten Abschnittes ergänzt.

* Minim in M.S.
Halbe Note in der Handschrift.

5.
(♮)
(♯)
(♯)
(♯)
(♯)
(♯)
6.
(♯)

7.
3
3
3
3
(♯)
(♯)
(♯)

8.

9.

10.
(♯)
9
4
11.

12.
(#)
WILLIAM BYRD.

LXI.
Monsieurs Alman.

WILLIAM BYRD.

* B' in the M. S.
B' in der Handschrift.

Rep.
2.

Rep.
(♯)
WILLIAM BYRD.

LXII.
Variatio.

WILLIAM BYRD.

* Quavers in M. S.
Achtel in der Handschrift.

2.

Rep.
2.

Rep.

2.
Rep.

(♯)
(♮)
(♯)
3
(♯)
(♯)
Rep.

2
Rep.
(#)
WILLIAM BYRD.

LXIII.
Alman.

WILLIAM BYRD.

2

3

4
WILLIAM BYRD.

LXIV.
Sellinger's Round.

WILLIAM BYRD.

3
4

5

* Quaver in M.S.
Achtel in der Handschrift.

* F in M.S.
F in der Handschrift.

9
(♯)
(♯)
WILLIAM BYRD.

LXV.
Fortune.

WILLIAM BYRD.

(♭)
(♭)
(#)
3
(♭)

4

* Semiquavers in M.S.
* Sechzehntel in der Handschrift.

LXVI.
O Mistris Myne.

WILLIAM BYRD.

* C sharp in M.S.
* Cis in der Handschrift.

* Semiquavers in M. S.
* Sechzehntel in der Handschrift.

— A crotchet and quaver in M. S.
— Viertel und Achtel in der Handschrift.

* Crotchet in M. S.
* Viertel in der Handschrift.

* Quavers in M. S.
* Achtel in der Handschrift.

LXVII.
The Woods so Wild.

WILLIAM BYRD.

2

3

4

5
6
7

8
9
10
11

WILLIAM BYRD. 1590.

LXVIII.
Walsingham.

WILLIAM BYRD.

(♮)
6
7
8

9
10
11

12
(♮)
(♮)
13
14
(♭)
(♭)
(♭)
(♭)
(♭)
(♯)
(♯)

* Crotchets in M.S.
Viertel in der Handschrift.

** Demisemiquavers in M.S.
Zweiunddreissigstel in der Handschrift.

*** Crotchet in M.S.
Viertel in der Handschrift.

* The G is a semibreve in the M.S.
Das G ist eine ganze Note in der Handschrift.

** Quavers in M.S.
Achtel in der Handschrift.

* Semiquavers in M. S.
Sechzehntel in der Handschrift.

LXIX.
The Bells.

WILLIAM BYRD

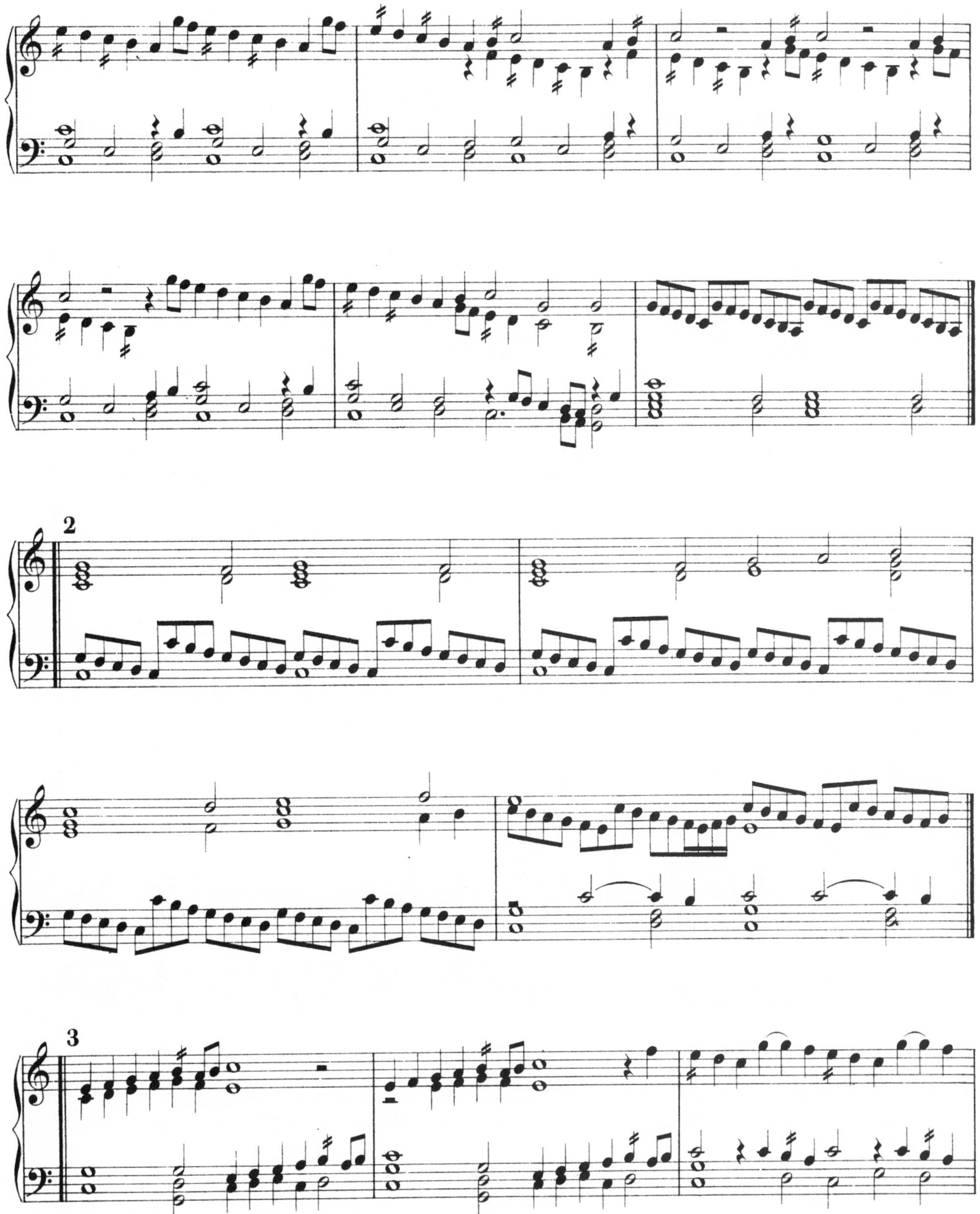
2
3

4
5
6

7
8

WILLIAM BYRD

LXX.

Tirsi. Di Luca Marenzio 1a Parte. Intavolata di Pietro Philippi.

1.

PETER PHILIPS.

(#) (#) (#) (#) (#)

* E in M S.
E in der Handschrift.

** Crotchet and quaver in M. S.
Viertel und Achtel in der Handschrift.

LXXI.
Freno. Seconda Parte.
2.

PETER PHILLIPS.

* Crotchet in M. S.
Viertel in der Handschrift.

* C, B, ♯A, B in M. S.
C, H, Ais, H in der Handschrift.

LXXII.
Cosi moriro.
3ª Parte.
3.

PETER PHILIPS.

PEETER PHILIPS.

LXXIII.
Fece da voi.
à 6.
4.

P. PHILIPS.

PEETER PHILIPS.

* Semiquavers in M. S.
16tel in der Handschrift.

LXXIV.
Pavana Pagget.
5.

PETER PHILIPS.

2
Rep.

** D in M. S.
D in der Handschrift.

* A F in M. S.
A F in der Handschrift.

Rep.

PEETER PHILIPS.

LXXV.
Galiarda.
6.

PETER PHILIPS.

Rep.
(♯) (♮)
(♮)
(♮)
3
(♯)(♮)

Rep.
(♯) (♮)
(♯) (♮) (♮) (♯)
PEETER PHILIPS.

LXXVI.
Passamezzo Pavana.
7.

PETER PHILIPS.

(♭) (♭) (♮) (♭) (♭) (♭) (♭) (♮) (♭)

2
3

4

* C in M.S.
C in der Handschrift.

* E in M. S.
E in der Handschrift.

6

* A in M.S.
A in der Handschrift.

** Another D here in M.S.
Noch ein D hier in der Handschrift.

LXXVII.
Galiarda Passamezzo.
8.

PETER PHILIPS.

8

[*]

(♮)

2

(♭)

(♭)

(♭)

(♭)

* Minim in M.S.
Halbe Note in der Handschrift.

* Minims in M.S.
Halbe Noten in der Handschrift.

5
6

* The notes F & A are in the M. S. above these chords.
Die Noten F und A stehen in der Handschrift über diesen Accorden.

* A in M.S.
A in der Handschrift.

PEETER PHILIPS.

LXXVIII.
Chi fara fede al Cielo, di Alessandro Striggio.
9.

PETER PHILIPS.

PETER PHILIPS.

LXXIX.
Bon Jour mõ Cueur di Orlando [di Lasso].
10.

PETER PHILIPS.

(♯)
(♯)
3
(♯)

PETER PHILIPS 1602.

LXXX.
Pauana Doloroso. Treg[ian].
11.

SET BY PETER PHILIPS.

(b) (b)

Rep.

(♯)

2
(♯)
(♯)

Rep.
(♯) (♯)
(♯ ♯)
(♯ ♯)

(♯)
(♯)
(♯)
3

PETER PHILIPS 1593.

LXXXI.
Galiarda Dolorosa.
12.

PETER PHILIPS.

* Quaver in M. S.
Achtel in der Handschrift.

** C in M. S.
C in der Handschrift.

* B in M. S.
H in der Handschrift.

* In the original madrigal this F is sharp.
Fis im Original-Madrigal.

** F in the M.S.
F in der Handschrift.

PETER PHILIPS 1603.

LXXXIII.
Margott Laborez.
14.

[Orlando di Lasso arranged by]
PETER PHILIPS.

PETER PHILIPS 1605.

LXXXIV.
Fantasia.
15.

PETER PHILIPS.

1 2 3 4 5 6

11
12
(♯)
(♯)
(♯)
13
4
(♯)
14
15

(♯)
16
17
18
19
(♯)
20
21
22
(♯)
24
23

25
26
(♯)
27
(♯)
28
R. H.
L. H.
(♯)
29

(♯)
(♯)
(♯)
30
(♯)
(♯)
(♯)
(♯)
31

32
33
34

35
36
37
38
39
PETER PHILIPS.

LXXXV.
Pavana.*
16.

PETER PHILIPS.

* In the margin are the words „The first one Philips made."
Eine Randbemerkung bezeichnet dieses Stück als Philips' erste Pavana.

2
Rep.

PETER PHILIPS. 1580.

LXXXVI.
Le Rossignuol.
17.

[Orlando di Lasso, set by]
PETER PHILIPS.

* G sharp in M. S.
Gis in der Handschrift.

* G in M.S.
G in der Handschrift.

(♭)
3

PETER PHILIPS. 1595.

LXXXVII.
Galliardo.
18.

PETER PHILIPS.

PETER PHILIPS.

LXXXVIII.
Fantasia.
19.

PETER PHILIPS.

PETER PHILIPS. 1582.

LXXXIX.
Fantasia.
1.

NICHOLAS STROGERS.

* C in MS.
C in der Handschrift.

NICHOLAS STROGERS.

* Quavers in M. S.
Achtel in der Handschrift.

XC.
Alman.

MARTIN PEERSON.

2
MARTIN PEERESON.

XCI.
Pavana. Bray.

WILLIAM BYRD.

2
Rep.

3

WILLIAM BYRD.

XCII.
Galiarda.

WILLIAM BYRD.

3 [6/2]

Rep.

2

Rep.

3

Rep.

WILLIAM BYRD.

XCIII.
Pavana. Ph. Tr.

WILLIAM BYRD.

Rep.

[1]

2

* F sharp in the M. S.
Fis in der Handschrift.

Rep.
6
6
WILLIAM BYRD.

XCIV.
Galiarda.

WILLIAM BYRD.

WILLIAM BYRD.

XCV.
Toccata.

GIOVANNI PICHI.

Giovanni Pichi.

[XCVI.]
Praeludium Toccata.
1.

J. P. SWEELINCK.

* Minim in the M.S.
Halbe Note in der Handschrift.

* The change of clef is omitted in the M.S.
Der Wechsel des Schlüssels fehlt in der Handschrift.

* A sharp is placed before the A in this chord.
In diesem Accorde steht ein Kreuz vor A.

JEHAN PIETERSON SWELLINCK.

[XCVII.]
Pavana.
1.

THOMAS WARROCK

* E♭ in M.S.
Es in der Handschrift.

3

* The middle note of the chord is D in the M. S.
Die mittlere Note dieses Accordes ist in der Handschrift D.

[XCVIII.]
Galiarda.
2.

THOMAS WARROCK.

Rep.
3

THOMAS WARROCK.

[XCIX]
Praeludium.
1.

GALEAZZO.

GALEAZZO

[C.]

Praeludium to y^e Fancie, Pag. 188. [Nº LII.]

WILLIAM BYRD.

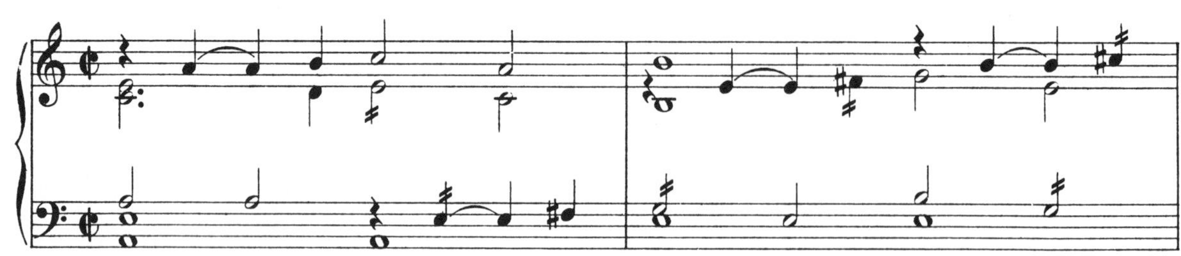

WILLIAM BYRD.

[CI.]
Ut, re mi, fa, sol, la.

WILLIAM BYRD.

* B in the M. S.
B in der Handschrift.

(♭)
4.
5.
(♭)
6.
(♯)
7.

8.
9.
10.
11.

12.
(♯)
13.

14.
15
16.

* The M S. has probably by an oversight.
In der Handschrift steht wahrscheinlich aus Versehen.

** This Latin direction seems to be the equivalent of our "attacca".
Diese lateinische Bezeichnung dürfte unserem „attacca" entsprechen.

[CII.]
Ut, mi, re.

WILLIAM BYRD.

8
(♯)
9.

10
11
12

* The M.S. has A in this chord.
In der Handschrift steht bei diesem Accorde A.

[CIII.]
Fantasia.

WILLIAM BYRD.

* B A in the M.S.
H A in der Handschrift.

(♯)
(♯)
L. H.

* E in the M. S.
E in der Handschrift.

WILLIAM BYRD.

[CIV]

All in a Garden green.

WILLIAM BYRD.

2

3
(♯)
4
(♯)
(♯)
(♯)
6
6

(♯)
(♯)
6
(♯)
5
(♯)
(♯)

6
(♯)
6
(♯)
6
(♯)
(♯)
WILLIAM BYRD.

[CV]
Heaven and Earth.

FRE. [qu. F. TREGIAN?]

6
FRE.

[CVI.]
Praeludium.

JOHN BULL.

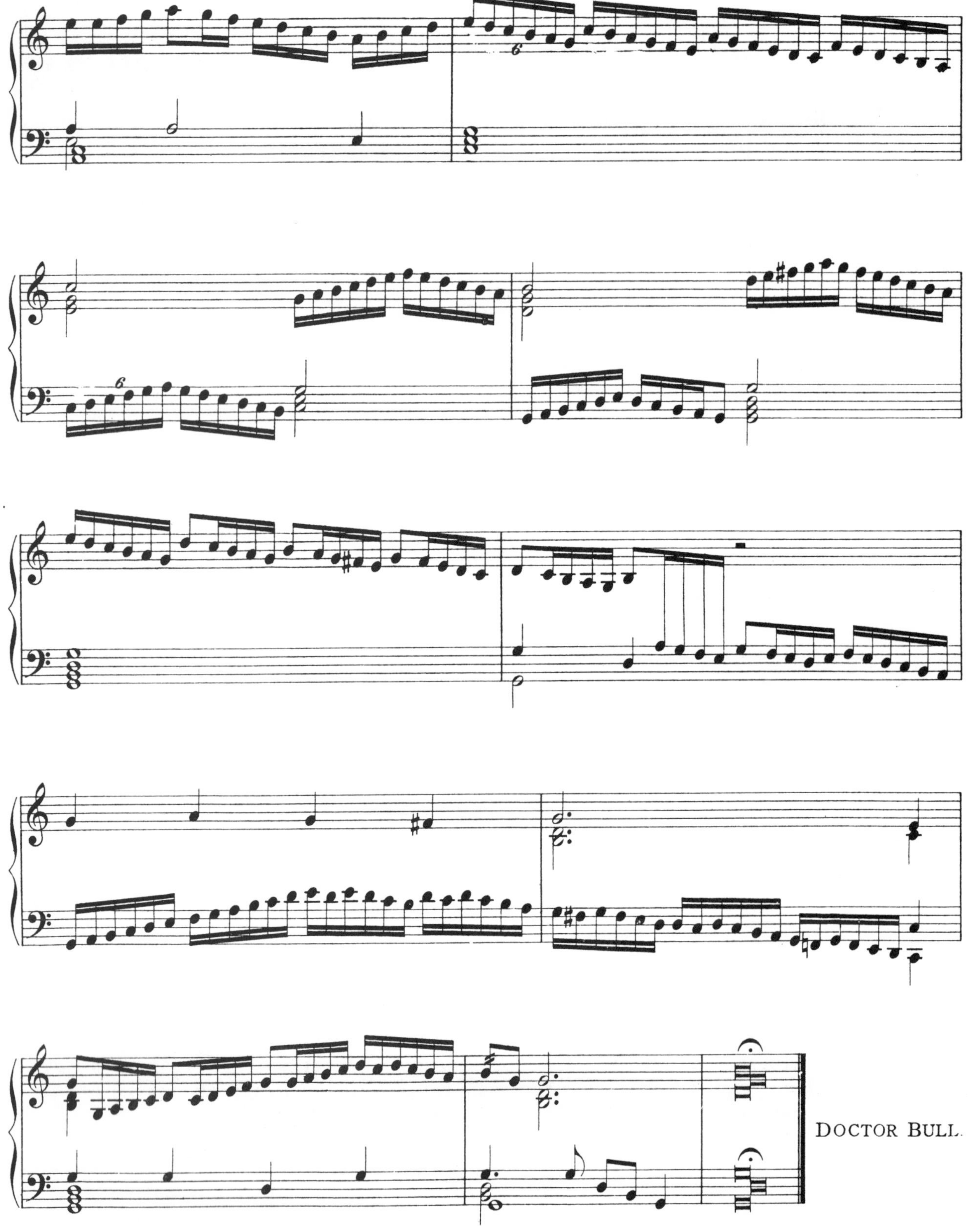
DOCTOR BULL.

[CVII.]
Veni.

ANON.

[CVIII.]
Fantasia.

JOHN BULL.

* A in M. S.
A in der Handschrift.

DOCTOR BULL.

[CIX.]
Felix namque.
I.

THOMAS TALLIS.

12
4
12
4

18
4

* A in the M.S.
A in der Handschrift.

THOMAS TALLIS. 1562.